$14.95 U.S.A.
$19.95 Canada

What do you do if during a worship service someone's cell phone rings? This could be an embarrassing position for every one, or it could be turned into a humorous situaton if the pastor says something like, "If that is God calling, tell him you are doubling your giving."

Or during a heavy downpour the pastor could say, "Isn't that just like God? Here we are inside praising His name, and He is outside washing our cars!"

In this book author Sidney Stone, a retired Baptist minister, shares 1000 ideas he gathered from his visits to over 500 churches of all denominations in the United States and Canada. These ideas range from coping situations to statements of belief, from sermons to outreach.

The author invites you to copy and use portions of the book in your bulletins, sermons, and belief statements.

1001 Fresh Ideas for Your Church

1001 Fresh Ideas for Your Church

Sidney Stone

Petros Publishers
P.O. Box 154
Hayward, California 94543

FIRST EDITION

ISBN 0-9715302-0-3
Published by
Petros Publishers
P.O. Box 154
Hayward, California 94543

Acknowledgements

Almost all of the 1001 ideas in this book came from my personal visits to more than 500 churches across the United States and Canada. You may recognize some of these ideas, for which I am indebted. All of the churches visited are arranged on the cover of this book, thanks to my friend, Ken Lester.

For encouragement, support, and contributions I wish to acknowledge my dear wife, Alice, my daughter, Carolyn, and my son, Dr. David Stone—and also the members of Genie Lester's Writers Group.

For their critiquing, proofreading, and ideas I thank my life-long friends from Eckert, Colorado, the Rev. William Kastning and his wife, Mary Ann; my pastor from Hayward, California, Dr. Dean Goddard; and poet Tammy Durston Billings, who gave good advice on marketing.

But the one person without whose help this book might never have been published is Genie Lester. Thank you, Genie, for your countless hours of research, suggestions, and formatting.

Dear readers, you have my permission to copy any portion of this book for your church bulletins, newsletters, bulletin boards, sermons, and statements of belief/missions. God bless you, and God bless America.

TABLE OF CONTENTS

FOREWORD

My relationship with Sidney Stone goes back seventeen years ago when I became his pastor. During that time I have found him to be generous and supportive and never critical. My conclusion about Sidney Stone is that he is an *aves rerara,* that is Latin for a "rare duck." He is an octogenarian whose mind is sharp and whose heart is warm for the work of Christ.

Sidney loves the Lord and His church. He is a friend of pastors and in favor of the church reaching the world for Jesus.

He has taken the time and trouble to do what no pastor could do. He has visited literally hundreds of churches and gathered hundreds of ideas for churches from all of his visits.

When he asked me to proofread his manuscript, I reluctantly agreed to do so thinking that it would be boring to read so many unrelated ideas. Instead, I found myself captivated and touched deeply by the continuity of truth running through so many ideas from so many different kinds of churches.

As a pastor I found many things here that I could use and will use. What man of God in his right mind would not pay the small price of this book for one good idea that could be used in his church, yet there are literally dozens of useful ideas. What's more, these ideas will create more ideas. They will focus the mind and heart of the pastor on his work and how he can improve it.

He who buys this book will be blessed; but he who does not, will miss out forever. The reader is the winner here. Surely by now you know, dear reader, that what you don't know can hurt you. Read and prosper!

Dean A. Goddard
Barachel on Burnham
Hayward, California

(Dr. Dean A. Goddard
Pastor, Liberty Christian Fellowship
Fremont, California)

PREFACE

All my life, over 65 years, I have attended churches of the same denomination. Then, after retiring from the pastoral ministry (the last church was the First Baptist Church of Livermore, California), I became interested in the worship services, programs, and outreach of other churches. I wanted to know how green the grass was on the other side of the denominational fence.

First the goal was to visit 100 churches, then 300, and finally 500 churches of all denominations to research this book. The churches are listed on the book cover and also alphabetically in the appendix. The title of the book was inspired by a sign at a large grocery store, "1001 Fresh Ideas For Your Shopping." The easy part was getting ideas on parking, welcoming of visitors, church facilities, organization, mottoes/slogans, statements of beliefs/purposes/mission, church bulletins, order of worship, offertory, Communion, music, prayer, activities, membership procedures, special services, etc. The difficult part was to reduce the number of ideas to 1001. Therefore I had to sub-divide some of the ideas.

In attending these churches I soon found exciting, unique, creative ideas that would have made my own ministry more effective. For example:

> **Idea # 129**, Have a large sign at the parking lot exit, **"NOW THE SERVICE BEGINS."**
>
> **Idea # 151**, Have a plaque over the drinking fountain, ***"Whosoever drinks of this water shall thirst again, but whosoever drinks of the water that I shall give him shall never thirst."***
>
> **Idea # 155**, Have a large replica of a butterfly near the cross to signify the resurrection.

I visited every denominational and non-denominational place of worship I could find—in the phone book, in newspapers, over the radio, by word-of-mouth, and by drive-by sightings. Most of the churches were in California; but other states visited included Florida, Kansas, Massachusetts, Missouri, Rhode Island, Texas, Virginia, Washington D.C., and also, in British Columbia, Vancouver and Barnaby..

In addition to the 1001 ideas, there are listed in the appendix 74 general slogans, 101 invitational slogans, 264 mission slogans, 312 identity slogans, as well as 154 bulletin board sayings. You may recognize some of these ideas and slogans, and I thank you for your contribution. I hope you will also benefit from the many ideas in the book. May your church grow not only in membership and outreach, but also in love for the Lord and one another.

CHAPTER 1

Slogans and Mottoes

The difference between a slogan and a motto is that a slogan is usually longer. They both are brief statements expressing a principle, a goal, or an ideal for a group (such as a church). Churches prefer one word over the other, but the intent is the same. A slogan or motto may be remembered long after the sermon is forgotten. Most churches I visited had the goal of the Great Commission, often in print, but condensed it to a slogan or motto.

Originally this chapter had 21 ideas, but they were reduced to nine, with sub-titled ideas to help keep the number down from over 2000 ideas to 1001.

Slogans and Mottoes

00l. Select one of the 74 General Slogans in the appendix,

or

002. Select one of the 312 Identity Slogans in the appendix,

or

003. Select one of the 101 Invitational Slogans in the appendix

or

004. Select one of the 264 Mission Slogans in the appendix,

and

a. have that slogan in the church bulletin,

and/or

b. have that slogan on a banner in the lobby, or narthex,

and/or

c. have the slogan given in a different language,

and/or

d. have a different member (with name in bulletin) give the slogan at the beginning of the service.

005. Have a member write a song about the slogan, especially if one is applicable to visitors.

006. Have a church motto, such as "I Refuse To Be Bound By Satan; For Jesus Has Made Me Free, And I Am Free Indeed."

007. Have a member write a song about the Church Motto.

008. Have different families rise and say the Church Motto. (Put their names in the bulletin.)

009. Have the congregation stand and recite the Motto.

CHAPTER 2
Belief Statements

All the churches I visited had statements of belief (faith, doctrines, essential beliefs). Many had them printed in the bulletin. The examples of individual churches in this chapter are reprinted as given, except for a few corrections in grammar and punctuation.

I contacted some 30 major denominations for their statements of faith and received replies from about half. Some of the ones we did receive were several pages; and if all the main denominations statements were forthcoming, that would be a book in itself.

This chapter on Belief Statements is still the longest in the book, and many of the statements are similar, only worded differently. Your church may find the wording most comfortable to you.

Belief Statements

010. A Word About Our Faith

- The Bible is the inspired Word of God.
- There is one God in three persons—Father, Son, and Holy Spirit.
- We believe in the deity of Jesus Christ, His virgin birth, His death, burial and resurrection.
- All men by nature are sinful and lost, need new birth for salvation.
- Men are justified by faith alone in the shed blood of Jesus Christ, not by personal works.
- Satan is a personal being, and Hell is a place of eternal punishment for the unsaved.
- We believe in the eternal security of the believer.
- The two scriptural ordinances of the church are believer's baptism and the Lord's Supper.
- Christians should live holy lives, separated from the world unto God.

011. A Word About Our Faith

We believe God loves us, as He has shown us through His Son, Jesus Christ. Jesus died on the cross and rose from the dead so that He can freely give forgiveness of sin and eternal life to those who believe in Him. His Holy Spirit is active in our world today.

Through the Bible God helps each one of us to know and experience how He wants us to live with Him and with each other. The Bible is our trustworthy authority on what to believe and how to walk with God.

Loving freedom guides us in living out our firm faith. People in our congregation are from many different backgrounds and appreciate the richness of our diversity in Christ.

Because we are followers of the Lord Jesus Christ, we are one in Him. We welcome into our church family all who confess Jesus Christ as Savior and Lord, as well as all who are seeking Him.

012. Affirmation of Faith

Leader: We Believe In The Father Who Is God Almighty,

Audience: The Creator Of All Things And The Preserver Of Light And Life.

Leader: We believe In The Son, Who Is Jesus Christ, God's Only Begotten Son.

Audience: He Was Human And Divine; Truly Lived, Suffered And Died, Rose Again From The Dead, Ascended On High, And Is Coming Again.

Leader: We Believe That Jesus Was Sent By God To Reveal God To Man .

Audience: That Whosoever Believeth In Him Shall Not Perish, But Have Everlasting Life.

Leader: We Believe In The Holy Ghost Who Was Sent From God The Father And The Son,

Audience: That The Holy Spirit Convicts And Converts Sinners, Dwells In The Believer, Keeps The Believer From The Power Of Sin And Leads Him To The Father Through His Son, Jesus Christ.

Leader: We Believe The Bible Is The Word Of God Given By Inspiration Through Holy Men.

Audience: That In The Bible God Seeks To Reveal His Will And Man Seeks To Respond To God's Revelation.

Leader: We Believe The Union Of The Father, Son And Holy Ghost Is Revealed Through His Church.

Audience: That All Believers Are United Into One Body, The Church.

Leader: We Believe That Christ Is Coming Back For His Holy Church Without Spot Or Wrinkle.

All: That Without Holiness In Spirit, Soul And Body, No Man Shall See The Lord!

013. Belief Statement

GOD—God is the creator and ruler of the universe. He has eternally existed in three personalities: the Father, the Son, and the Holy Spirit. These three personalities: the Father, the Son and the Holy Spirit are co-equal and are one God.
Gen. 1:1; Gen. 1:26-27; Psalm 90:2; Matt. 28:19; I Pet. 1:2; 2 Cor. 13:14
JESUS CHRIST—Jesus Christ is the Son of God. Jesus lived a sinless human life and offered Himself as the perfect sacrifice for the sins of all people by dying on the cross. He rose from the dead after three days to demonstrate his power over sin and death. He ascended to Heaven's glory and will return some day to earth to reign forever.
Matt. 1:22; John 1:1-5; John 14:10-13; Heb. 4:14-15; I Cor. 15:3-4; Rom. 1:3-4; Acts 1:9-11; I Tim. 6:14-15; Titus 2:13
HOLY SPIRIT—The Holy Spirit is God's presence in the world today. He is present to make people aware of their need for Jesus Christ. He lives in every Christian from the moment of salvation to provide power for living and understanding of spiritual truth and guidance in doing what is right. He guarantees the believer's salvation, and gives spiritual gifts for the purpose of ministry.
John 14:16-17; John 16:7-13; Acts 1:8; I Cor. 2:12; 3:16; Eph 1:13-14; Eph. 5:18; I Cor. 12:4-7

014. Beliefs

Here are examples of distinctive beliefs that are familiar to most Christians but receive special emphasis in our church:

• We believe God's Spirit is available to guide us today, both as individuals in our daily lives and as a church through prophetic leadership and an open canon of scripture.

• We believe in a priesthood that is called of God by revelation through an administrative structure in which the man or woman accepts specific responsibilities of service. The offices of priesthood are found in the Scriptures. Examples: prophet, apostle, high priest, evangelist, bishop, seventy, elder, priest, teacher, deacon.

• We believe in stewardship, which means we accept God as creator of our universe and everything in it. We are stewards over creation, including our own bodies and minds, the earth on which we live, and the blessings we receive. We feel we are accountable to God for our stewardship response to the opportunities placed before us to grow and develop.

015. Because We Believe

- We believe in God the Father.
- We believe in Christ the Son.
- We believe in the Holy Spirit.
- We are the Church and we stand as one.
- We believe in the Holy Bible.
- We believe in the Virgin Birth.
- We believe in the Resurrection.
- We believe that Christ one day will return to Earth.

016. Confession Of Faith

(1) We believe that the Bible is the Word of God. As such, it is fully trustworthy in all it teaches and affirms. II Timothy 3:16; II Peter 1:20-21

(2) We believe in one eternal God who exists as Father, Son and Holy Spirit. Mark 12:29; I Timothy 3:16

(3) We believe that our Lord Jesus Christ was begotten, not created, truly God, truly man. John 3:16; John 1:1, 14

(4) We believe that all men are fallen (sin nature) and cannot be saved except through faith in the death and resurrection of Christ. Therefore, we speak of the "new birth" as a radical spiritual transformation when the old life is put away and new life in Christ is received. II Cor. 5:17; Eph 2:8

(5) We believe that Jesus had given the church ordinances of water baptism to be administered in His name, and the Lord's Supper (Communion) for the believer's identification with His life, death, and resurrection. Acts 2:38: I Cor. 11:23-26

(6) We believe in the literal and the imminent return of Jesus Christ to this earth. I Thess. 4:16,17; Acts 1:11

(7) We believe in the spiritual unity of all who are born of God. We confess even those Christ followers with whom we disagree, those who do not confess us, and others whom we exclude because of our unwillful ignorance. Rom 10:12; John 17-2

(8) We believe that those who are called by the name of Christ should seek to live a godly life. Understanding that salvation from the penalty of sin only begins the process of redemption, we acknowledge that one work of the Holy Spirit is to create in us the character of Christ. I Cor. 6:189-20; I John 5:2

017. Our Beliefs

The Scriptures Inspired

The Scriptures are inspired by God. They provide the revelation of God to man and are every Christian's infallible, authoritative rule of faith and conduct. The Bible stands alone as our text, showing us what to believe and how to live.

The One True God

The One True God has revealed Himself as the eternally self-existent "I AM", the Creator of heaven and earth, and the Redeemer of mankind. He has further revealed Himself as Father, Son, and Holy Spirit. These three persons in the Godhead are in a state of unity. There is one Lord, God Almighty.

Jesus Christ

Jesus is fully God and fully man. He was born of a virgin, lived His earthly life a perfect example, and gave His life as the perfect sacrifice for the sins of the world. We believe that Jesus died for our sins according to the Scripture as a representative and substitutionary sacrifice, and that all who believe in Him are justified on the ground of His shed blood. We believe in the resurrection of the crucified body of our Lord, His ascension into Heaven, and His present life as High Priest and Advocate.

The Holy Spirit

The Holy Spirit is the Comforter who dwells in the hearts of Christians convincing them of truth and convicting them of sin. He gives each believer spiritual gifts to be developed and used in worship and in ministry.

About Man

Man was created good and upright, for God said, "Let us make man in our image, after our likeness." However, man, by voluntary transgression, fell into sin and thereby incurred not only physical death, but also spiritual death, which is separation from God. Man's only hope of redemption is through the shed blood of Jesus Christ. Salvation is received through repentance toward God and faith in the Lord Jesus Christ.

The Church

We believe that all who are born of the Holy Spirit belong to the one true Church. The Church is the Body of Christ, the habitation of God through the Spirit. Jesus Christ is the head of the Church.

The Blessed Hope

We believe in "the blessed hope," the personal and imminent return of our Lord and Savior Jesus Christ. We believe in the bodily resurrection of the just and of the unjust; the everlasting reward of the saved, and the everlasting conscious punishment of the lost.

Prayer

We believe in the power of prayer in the believer's life. We are instructed in the Scriptures to ask God to work sovereignly in our lives. We believe that God's power is still at work in this world to bring healing to the sick.

Sacraments

We have two sacraments instituted by Christ. They are believer's baptism and holy communion. We believe that every believer should obey the Lord's instruction to participate in these sacraments. Baptism identifies us publicly with Christ in His death, burial, and resurrection. Communion causes us to remember the sacrifice Christ made on our behalf.

018. Our Beliefs, Mission, and Vision

We hold the Bible to be the inspired Word of God, the rule Book for Life, which presents Jesus Christ, God's only begotten Son, whose death and bodily resurrection provide forgiveness from sin and eternal life to any and all who receive Him by faith. Christ's indwelling presence through the Holy Spirit gives power and purpose to our lives. It is the Christian's duty and privilege to give this message of hope to the whole world until the bodily return of Jesus Christ for the establishment of His Kingdom.

Our mission is to reach as many people as possible, through as many means possible, to experience a personal relationship with Jesus Christ; and in turn, to disciple each one of them through a variety of ways to reach others for Jesus Christ. Simply stated, we seek to reach, to teach, and to reach again.

Our vision is to reach our world for Jesus Christ. We desire nothing short of uniting with God and His many servants the world over to fulfill the great commandment of Jesus Christ:

> *Go, therefore, and make disciples of all the nations, baptizing them in the name of the Father and the Son and the Holy Spirit, teaching them to observe all that I commanded you; and lo, I am with you always, even to the end of the age.* Matthew 28:19-20

This begins by reaching out to the community in which God has uniquely placed us, and then further to the whitened harvest field around the world.

019. Our Distinctive Values

Christ-Centered. We believe that the greatest need of all people is a personal relationship with Jesus Christ. The Bible teaches how this relationship permeates every aspect of one's life.

Relationship-Focused. We believe that loving relationships should be developed and maintained in every aspect of church life.

Organized by Gifting. We believe that the church should operate as a fully-functioning community, each person ministering according to the gifts God has given them, regardless of race, gender, age, or marital status.

Small Groups. We believe that life-change happens best in small groups. We also believe that it is in this context that Christ's followers minister best to one another.

Seeker-Sensitive. We believe in making the gospel accessible to people without a church background by using methods which remove barriers and build bridges to their understanding of the gospel message. We believe in allowing seekers to investigate Christianity at their own pace.

Relevant to Culture. We believe the church should be culturally relevant while remaining doctrinally pure. This will be reflected in a contemporary worship style, practical messages, use of the arts, etc.

Outward Focused. We believe that lost people matter to God and therefore ought to matter to the church. We believe that the church should reach out to lost people in relationships and activities.

Authentic. We believe that authentic growth takes place in a climate of acceptance and transparency in relationships. We believe the church should help people to reach their full potential by addressing the needs of the whole person.

Devoted to God's Mission. We believe that full devotion to God and His mission is normal for every believer. This includes being involved in ministry and the investment of one's resources.

Standard of Excellence. We believe that excellence honors God and inspires people. We believe in the continuous evaluation and improvement of all aspects of the church.

020. Our Distinctives

We believe that:

The Bible, God's only inspired and inerrant word, is our standard of faith and practice.

The new birth by faith in Jesus Christ through grace alone is absolutely necessary and lasts forever.

A church is composed of born again believers only.

A church is governed by the congregation under Christ as its Head.

Believers are priests responsible to worship the Triune God everywhere.

Baptism is by immersion in water after salvation.

Separation from the world is essential to the individual for personal holiness.

Separation of church and state is essential to the Church for freedom from governmental interference.

A church has Scriptural offices (Pastor, Deacons, and Deaconesses) and two ordinances (Baptism and the Lord's Supper).

021. Our Statement Of Faith

(1) About God. God is the Creator and Ruler of the universe. He has eternally existed in three persons; the Father, the Son, and the Holy Spirit. These three are co-equal and are one God.
Genesis 1:1, 26,27; 3:22; Psalm 90:2; Matthew 28:19; I Peter 1:2, II Corinthians 13:14

(2) About Mankind. We are all made in the spiritual image of God, to be like Him in character. We are the supreme object of God's creation. Although mankind has tremendous potential for good, we are marred by an attitude of disobedience toward God called "sin." This attitude separates us from God.
Genesis 1:27; Psalm 8-3-6; Isaiah 53:6a; Romans 3:23; Isaiah 59:1,2

(3) About Eternity. We were created to exist forever. We will either exist eternally separated from God by sin, or in union with God through forgiveness and salvation. The place of eternal separation from God is called Hell. Heaven is the place of eternal union and eternal life with God.
John 3:15; Romans 6:23; Revelation 20:15 [Hell]; Matthew 25:41; Revelation 21:27 [Heaven]

(4) About Jesus Christ. Jesus Christ is the Son of God. He is co-equal with the Father. Jesus lived a sinless human life and offered Himself as the perfect sacrifice for the sins of all by dying on a cross. He arose from the dead after three days to demonstrate His power over sin and death. He ascended to Heaven's glory and will return again to earth to reign as King of Kings, and Lord of Lords. (Matthew 1:22,23; Isaiah 9:6;I John 1:1-5; John 14:10-30; Hebrews 4:14,15; I Corinthians 15:3,4; Romans 1:3,4; Acts 1:9-11; I Timothy 6:14,15; Titus 2:13)

(5) About Salvation. Salvation is a gift from God to mankind. We can never make up for our sin by self-improvement or good works. Only by trusting in Jesus Christ as God's offer of forgiveness can we be saved from sin's penalty. Eternal life begins the moment we receive Jesus Christ into our life by faith. (Romans 6:23; Ephesians 2:8,9; John 14:6; I John 1:12;I Titus 3; Galatians 3:26: Romans 5:I)

(6) About the Bible. The Bible is God's word to all mankind. It was written by human authors, under the supernatural guidance of the Holy Spirit. It is the supreme source of truth for Christian beliefs and living. Because it is inspired by God, it is truth without any mixture of error. (II Timothy 3:16; II Peter 1:20,21; II Timothy 1:13; Psalm 12:6; 119:105,106; Proverbs 30:5)

(7) About the Holy Spirit. The Holy Spirit is equal with the Father and the Son as God. He is present in the world to make mankind aware of our need for Jesus Christ. He also lives in every Christian from the moment of salvation. He provides the Christian with power for living, understanding of spiritual truth, and guidance in doing what is right. The Christian seeks to live under His control daily. (II Corinthians 3:17; John 1:16, 17; John 16:7-13; Acts1:8; Ephesians 5:1; I Corinthians 2:12, 3:16; Ephesians 1:13; Galatians 5:23)

022. We Believe...

The Bible is the inspired and only infallible and authoritative written Word of God.

...there is one God, eternally existent in three persons: God the Father, God the Son, and God the Holy Ghost.

...in the deity of our Lord Jesus Christ, in His virgin birth, in His sinless life, in His miracles, in His vicarious and atoning death, in His bodily resurrection, in His ascension to the right hand of the Father, in His personal future return to this earth in power and glory to rule a thousand years.

023. Our Statement Of Faith

• We believe the Bible as God's inspired and inerrant Word is of final authority in faith and life.

• We believe, based on this Word, in one God, existing eternally in three Persons: God the Father, God the Son, and God the Holy Spirit.

• We believe Jesus Christ was begotten of the Holy Spirit and is true God and true man.

• We believe the Holy Spirit convicts of sin, makes believers children of God through new birth, assures believers of their salvation; and by His indwelling presence, enables believers to live a godly life.

• We believe man was created in God's image, but sinned, incurring spiritual death which has passed upon all the race.

• We believe that Christ died for our sins, according to the Scriptures, and that all who trust Him are justified on the ground of His shed blood.

• We believe in the resurrection of the Lord Jesus Christ and His present ministry in Heaven for us.

• We believe the personal, pre-millennial return of Christ is our "blessed hope".

• We believe in the bodily resurrection of the just and the unjust, the everlasting blessedness of the saved and the conscious everlasting punishment of the lost.

024. Our Statement Of Essential Beliefs

In essential beliefs--we have unity. *"There is one Body and one Spirit…there is one Lord, one faith, one baptism, and one God and Father of us all…"* Ephesians 4:4-6.

In non-essential beliefs--we have freedom. *"Accept him whose faith is weak, without passing judgment on disputable matters…Who are you to judge someone else's servant? To his own master he stands or falls…So then each of us will give an account of himself to God…So whatever you believe about these things keep between yourself and God."* Romans 14:1,4,12,22

In all our beliefs-we show love. *"…If I hold in my mind not only all human knowledge but also the very secrets of God, and if I have the faith that can move mountains-but have no love, I amount to nothing at all."* I Corinthians 13:2

025. The Essentials We Believe:

(1) About God. God is the Creator and Ruler of the Universe. He has eternally existed in three personalities: the Father, the Son, and the Holy Spirit. These three are co-equal and are one God. He loves all people and desires that they follow and worship Him alone. Genesis 1:1,26,27; 3:22; Psalm 90:2; Matthew 28:19; I Peter 1:2; II Corinthians 13:14

(2) About Jesus Christ. Jesus Christ is the Son of God. He is co-equal with the Father. Jesus lived a sinless human life and offered Himself as the perfect sacrifice for the sins of all people by dying on a cross. He rose from the dead to demonstrate His power over sin and death. He ascended to Heaven's glory and will return again to reign with power and glory. Matthew 1:22,23; Isaiah 9:6; I John 1:1-5, 14:10-30; Hebrews 4:14,15; I Corinthians 15:3,4; Romans 1:3,4; Acts 1:9-11; I Timothy 6:14,15; Titus 2:13

(3) About the Holy Spirit. The Holy Spirit is co-equal with the Father and the Son of God. He is present in the world to make people aware of their need for Jesus Christ. He also lives in every Christian from the moment of conversion. He provides the Christian with power for living, understanding of spiritual truth, and guidance in doing what is right. He gives every believer a spiritual gift when they are saved. As Christians we seek to live under His control daily.

(4) About the Bible. The Bible is God's Word to us. It was written by human authors, under the supernatural guidance of the Holy Spirit. It is the supreme source of truth for Christian beliefs and living. Because it is inspired by God, it is the truth without error.

(5) About Human Beings. People are made in the spiritual image of God, to be like Him in character. People are the supreme object of God's creation. Although every person has tremendous potential for good, all of us are marred by disobedience toward God called "sin". Sin separates people from God and causes many problems in life. Genesis 1:27; Psalm 8:3-6; Isaiah 53:6a; Romans 3:23; Isaiah 59:1, 2

(6) About Salvation. While salvation is God's free gift to us, we must take action to accept it. We can never make up for our sin by self-improvement or good works. Only by trusting in Jesus Christ as God's offer of forgiveness can anyone be saved from sin's penalty of eternal death. Romans 6:23; Ephesians 2:8,9; John 14:6, 1:12; Titus 3:5; Galatians 3:26; Romans 5:1

(7) About Eternal Security. Because God gives us eternal life through Jesus Christ, the true believer is secure in that salvation for eternity. If you have been genuinely saved, you cannot "lose" your gift of eternal life. Salvation is maintained by the grace and power of God, not by the effort of the Christian. It is the grace and power of God that gives us this security. John 10:29,30; II Timothy 1:12; Hebrews 7:25,10:10,14; I Peter 1:3-5

(8) About Eternity. Each of us will either exist eternally separated from God in torment, or eternally with God in glory. To be eternally separated from God is Hell. To be eternally in union with Him is eternal life. Heaven and Hell are real places of eternal existence. John 3:16; I John 14:17; Romans 6:23; Romans 8:17-18; Revelation 20:15; I Corinthians 2:7-9

(9) About The Church. There is no strict set of beliefs which separates (name of church) from other followers of Christ in other churches. We believe in being united with other Christians from our local church and being united with Christians from around the world who follow Him and obey God's Word, the Bible.

026. Our Statement Of Faith

We hold the Bible to be the inspired Word of God. It is the Book of Life which presents Jesus Christ, God's only Son, as man's Savior. By Jesus' death and bodily resurrection He has provided forgiveness from sin, and by the indwelling of the Holy Spirit gives newness of life. We believe that Jesus is our Healer, that He has called us by the Holy Spirit to spread the "good news" until the bodily return of Jesus Christ to this earth for the establishment of His Kingdom as our Coming King.

027. Profession Of Faith

We believe in one God, the Father, the Almighty, maker of heaven and earth, of all that is seen and unseen.

We believe in one Lord, Jesus Christ, the only Son of God, eternally begotten of the Father, God from God, Light from Light, true God from true God, begotten, not made, One in Being with the Father. Through Him all things were made. For us men and for our salvation He came down from heaven; by the power of the Holy Spirit, He was born of the Virgin Mary and became man. For our sake He was crucified under Pontius Pilate; He suffered, died, and was buried. On the third day He rose again in fulfillness of the Scriptures; He ascended into heaven and is seated at the right hand of the Father. He will come again in glory to judge the living and the dead, and His kingdom will have no end.

We believe in the Holy Spirit, the Lord, the giver of life, Who proceeds from the Father and the Son. With the Father and the Son He is worshipped and glorified. He has spoken through the Prophets. We believe in one holy catholic and apostolic Church. We acknowledge one baptism for the forgiveness of sins. We look for the resurrection of the dead and the life of the world to come. Amen.

028. We Believe

Our church exists to sincerely love God, share that love with others and participate in God's mission for the world. Jesus said that the greatest commandment is to *"Love the Lord your God...and to love your neighbor as yourself."* Matthew 22:37-38 We believe the most important thing we can do is to help people discover how to have a personal and growing relationship with God, and healthy relationships with others. Our Celebration Service and all of our ministries are designed to accomplish that purpose.

We believe that God loves all people and has a wonderful plan for their lives. We believe that we can discover that plan and answers to life's questions from the Bible. It is the foundation for our beliefs.

029. We Believe

The purpose of writing this statement of beliefs for (name of) Church is to identify a spirit of unity by declaring the common doctrinal understandings of the church. In doing this it will also serve as a reference point where opinions differ and provide a basis for doctrinal discussion in admitting members into the (name of) Church. It does provide a doctrinal guide to those who are examining this church for the purpose of participation in membership. The following then are the basic doctrinal beliefs of the (name of) Church:

(1) We believe that every human being has direct relations with God and is responsible to God alone in all matters of faith; that each church is independent and must be free from any ecclesiastical or political authority; that, therefore, church and state must be kept separate and having different functions and each fulfilling its duties free from dictation or patronage of the other. Romans 13 & 14:12

(2) We believe that the Bible is the Word of God, fully inspired and without error in the original manuscripts, written under the inspiration of the Holy Spirit, and that it has supreme authority in all matters of faith and conduct. II Timothy 3:16-17; Psalms 19:7; II Peter 1:2-21

(3) We believe in one living and true God, perfect in wisdom, sovereignty, holiness, justice, mercy and love. I Timothy 1:17; Psalms 86:15; Deuteronomy 32:3-4 He exists eternally in three co-equal persons who act together in creation, providence and redemption. Genesis 1:26; I Peter 1:2; Hebrews 1:1-3

a. We believe in God the Father, as infinite, personal Spirit, perfect in holiness, wisdom, power and love. We believe that He concerns Himself mercifully in the affairs of men, that He hears and answers prayer, that He saves from sin and death all who come to Him through Jesus Christ. John 2:24; Isaiah 44:6

b. We believe in Jesus Christ, God's only begotten Son, conceived by the Holy Spirit. We believe in His Virgin Birth, sinless life, miracles and teachings. We believe in His substitutionary atoning death for the sins of all people, bodily resurrection for empowering of the new life of all who believe, ascension into heaven, perpetual intercession for His people, and personal, visible return to earth. John 1:1-2; John 1:14; Romans 5:8; Luke 24:39; I Corinthians 15:3-4; Acts 1:11; Hebrews 7:25; I John 2:1; John 14:3

c. We believe in the Holy Spirit who came forth from the Father and Son to convict the world of sin, righteousness and judgment and to regenerate, sanctify, fill and empower all who believe in Jesus Christ; and that He wants to fill us and be our abiding helper, teacher and guide. I Corinthians 6:19; John 14:16-18; John 16:7-14; Acts 1:8; Ephesians 5:18; Galatians 5:16, 22-25

(4) We believe that all men are sinners by nature and choice, and we are therefore under just condemnation. We believe that those who repent of their sins and trust in Jesus Christ as Savior are regenerated by the Holy Spirit. We believe that they become a new creation in Christ Jesus, but the old nature is not eradicated. John 3:3-7; 3:16, 18; John 1:12-13; Romans 3:10, 23; 6:23; 10:9- 13; I Peter 1:18-19, 23

(5) We believe in the universal church, a living spiritual body of which Christ is the head and all regenerated persons are members. We believe in the local church, consisting of a

profession of faith and associated for worship, work and fellowship. We believe that God has laid upon the members of the local church that primary task of giving the gospel of Jesus Christ to a lost world. We believe that the Scriptural method of raising funds for the church is by means of the local tithe and free-will offerings. Acts 2:41; Colossians 1:18; Matthew 28:19-20; Ephesians 1:22, 23; I Corinthians 16:1-2

(6) We believe that a Christian should live for the glory of God and the well-being of his fellow men; that his conduct should be blameless before the world; that he should realize for himself and others the full status of maturity in Christ. 1 Corinthians 10-23, 31; I Corinthians 6:19-20; II Corinthians 6:14-18; II Peter 3:14; I Peter 2:9-10

(7) We believe that the Lord Jesus Christ has committed two ordinances to the local church: Baptism and the Lord's Supper. We believe that Christian baptism is the immersion of a believer into water in the name of the triune God. We believe that the Lord's Supper was instituted by Christ for commemoration of His death and remembrance of His return. We believe that these two ordinances should be observed and administered until the return of the Lord Jesus Christ. Matthew 26:26-29; 28:19; Romans 6:1- 11; I Corinthians 11:23-34; Acts 2:38

(8) We believe in the personal, visible return of the Lord Jesus Christ to earth and the establishment of His kingdom. We believe in the resurrection of the body, the final judgment, the eternal felicity of the righteous and everlasting suffering of the wicked. I Thessalonians 4:14-18; Isaiah 24; Revelation 20-22; Matthew 24-25; Acts 1:11

030. Statement Of Doctrine

(1) The Bible—Every word in the original writings of the Holy Scriptures is inspired of God, authoritative, and without error. The Bible is the only written revelation of God to man and is infallible.
(2) The Godhead—There is one God, existing eternally in three persons: Father, Son, and Holy Spirit. God is a Spirit, infinite, eternal and unchangeable.
(3) Jesus Christ—The Lord Jesus is the eternal Son of God. He entered the human race miraculously by being born of a virgin. He did not sin and He could not sin. He died as a substitute for all the sins of the human race, and buried, rose bodily from the grave and ascended to the Father's right hand where He now ministers as our

Great High Priest and Advocate. He is coming a second time, personally and visibly, to establish His worldwide kingdom on earth, and to take His church to be eternally with Him in heaven.

(4) The Holy Spirit—The Holy Spirit convicts and converts and comforts people. He regenerates, indwells, baptizes and seals all true believers in Christ and empowers them to live a holy life.

(5) Man—Adam was created in the image and likeness of God, and was an innocent being. He subsequently sinned and as head of the human race, he passed on a sinful nature to all mankind. All men are sinners by nature, but also by practice. Apart from God's salvation, man is lost eternally.

(6) Sin—Sin is violation of, or disobedience to the revealed will of God. It is also a state, the absence of righteousness, or anything that falls short of the perfect glory of God. God has established that the penalty for sin is eternal death.

(7) Salvation—Without the shedding of blood by the Lord Jesus, there is no remission of sin. Eternal salvation is by grace through faith in the Lord Jesus Christ and entirely apart from keeping the law or doing good works. It is entered into by all those who hear and understand the gospel, repent of their sin, and trust in Jesus Christ alone as their Lord and Savior.

(8) The Church—The universal church is made up of all true believers in the Lord Jesus from Pentecost to the Rapture. Each local church should be a miniature of the universal church, expressing the great truths of the latter. The local church is made up of believers in the Lord Jesus who have been baptized following their conversion and who meet together for teaching, fellowship, breaking of bread, prayer and evangelism. Christ is the Head of each local church and He entrusts leadership to the elders—men who are recognized as Christ's undershepherds. Each local church is to have deacons and deaconesses who serve the practical needs of the church.

(9) Ordinances—There are two and only two Christian ordinances: Baptism and the Lord's Supper. Baptism by immersion signifies that the believer has died with Christ, has been buried with Him, and has risen to walk in newness of life with Him. The Lord's Supper is a memorial feast at which believers worship the Lord and show forth His death until He comes again. In accordance with the early church, the Lord's Supper should be celebrated regularly.

(10) The Future—Jesus Christ is coming again at a time known only to God. Those who have died in Christ will be raised; those who are alive in Christ at His coming will be changed; and together they will be with Christ eternally. All who reject Christ as Lord and Savior will be judged and eternally punished.

031. Statement Of Faith

(1) We believe the Bible to be the inspired, the only infallible, authoritative Word of God.
(2) We believe there is one God eternally existent in three persons: Father, Son, and Holy Spirit.
(3) We believe in the Deity of the Lord Jesus Christ, in His virgin birth, in His sinless life, in His miracles, in His vicarious atoning death through His shed blood, in His bodily resurrection, in His ascension to the right hand of the Father and in His personal return in power and glory.
(4) We believe that for the salvation of lost and sinful man regeneration by the Holy Spirit is absolutely essential.
(5) We believe in the present ministry of the Holy Spirit by whose indwelling the Christian is enabled to live a godly life.
(6) We believe in the resurrection of both the saved and the lost; they that are saved unto the resurrection of life and they that are lost unto the resurrection of damnation.
(7) We believe in the spiritual unity of believers in our Lord Jesus Christ.

032. Statement Of Faith

A. We believe the Bible to be the inspired and only infallible authoritative Word of God. II Timothy 3:16
B. We believe that there is one God, eternally existent in three persons: Father, Son, and Holy Spirit. I John 5:6-8
C. We believe in the deity of our Lord Jesus Christ, in His virgin birth, in His sinless life, in His miracles, in His vicarious and atoning death through His shed blood, and His bodily resurrection, in His ascension to the right hand of the Father, and in His personal return in power and glory. I Corinthians 15:3-4; I Peter 2:18-24; John 3:126; Luke 1
D. We believe that for salvation of lost and sinful man regeneration by the Holy Spirit is absolutely essential. Romans 3:21-30; Galatians 4:4-7
E. We believe it is important, upon confession of Jesus Christ as Lord and Savior, to be water baptized. Matthew 28:18-20; Mark 16:15-16; Acts 8:35-39
F. We believe that the Baptism of the Holy Ghost for believers is evidenced by the initial sign of speaking with other tongues as the Spirit gives utterance and by the subsequent manifestation of spiritual power in public testimony and service. Acts 2:4; Acts 10:44-46; Acts 19:2; Acts 1:8; Acts 2:42-43; Matthew 3:11

G. We believe that deliverance from sickness is provided for in the atonement, and is the privilege of all believers. Isaiah 53:4; Matthew 8:16-17; Mark 16:18; John 5:6-14; and I Peter 2:24

H. We believe in the resurrection of both the saved and the lost: they who are saved unto the resurrection of life, and they who are lost unto the resurrection of damnation. John 5:24, 28 and 29

I. We believe in the imminent return of our Lord and Savior Jesus Christ. I Thessalonians 4:13-18; Revelation 22:20, and John 14:3

033. Statement Of Faith

We Believe the Bible to be the inspired and only infallible Word of God. We believe that there is one God eternally existent in Three Persons, God the Father, God the Son, God the Holy Spirit.

We Believe in the blessed hope, which is in the rapture of the Church of God which is in Christ at His return.

We Believe that the only means of being cleansed from sin is through repentance, faith in the precious Blood of Jesus Christ and being baptized in water. We believe that regeneration by the Holy Ghost is absolutely essential for personal salvation.

We Believe that the redemptive work of Christ on the cross provides healing for the human body in answer to believing prayer.

We Believe that the baptism in the Holy Ghost, according to Acts 2:4 is given to believers who ask for it.

We Believe in the sanctifying power of the Holy Spirit by whose indwelling the Christian is enabled to live a holy and separated life in this present world. Amen.

034. Statement Of Faith

We believe the only true basis of Christian fellowship is Christ's (Agape) love, which is greater than any differences we possess, and without which we have no right to claim ourselves Christians.

We believe worship of God should be spiritual. Therefore, we remain flexible and yielding to the leading of the Holy Spirit to direct our worship.

We believe worship of God should be inspirational. Therefore, we give great pleasure to music in our worship.

We believe worship of God should be intelligent. Therefore, our services are designed with great emphasis upon the teaching of the Word of God, that He might instruct us on how He should be worshipped.

We believe worship of God should be fruitful. Therefore, we look for His love in our lives as the supreme manifestation that we have been truly worshiping Him.

We believe in the inerrancy of Scripture, that the Bible, Old and New Testaments, in the original autographs, is the inspired, infallible Word of God, a complete and final written revelation of God.

We believe in one personal, transcendent, and holy God, the creator of all, Who is eternal, and Who manifests Himself in three separate persons: Father, Son and Holy Spirit.

We believe that Jesus Christ, though fully God, became a man for the suffering of death, that He is the promised Messiah, born of a virgin, lived a sinless life, provided for the atonement of our sins by His vicarious death on the Cross, was bodily resurrected by the power of the Holy Spirit, ascended back to the right hand of God the Father, and ever lives to make intercession for us.

We believe that after Jesus ascended to Heaven, He poured out His Holy Spirit on the believers in Jerusalem, enabling them to fulfill His command to preach the Gospel to the entire world, an obligation shared by all believers today.

We believe that all people are by nature separated from God and responsible for their own sin, but that salvation, redemption, and forgiveness are freely offered to all by the grace of our Lord Jesus Christ. When a person repents of sin and accepts Jesus Christ as personal Savior and Lord, trusting Him to save, that person is immediately born again and sealed by the Holy Spirit, all his or her sins are forgiven, and that person becomes a child of God.

We believe in the person and work of the Holy Spirit who indwells, seals, and empowers every believer, baptizing them into the Body of Christ. We further believe that the Holy Spirit will come upon any believer who asks in faith, enabling him or her to preach the Gospel in power. We also believe all of the gifts of the Holy Spirit mentioned in the Scriptures are valid for today if they are exercised within the scriptural guidelines. We believe that love is more important than all the gifts, and without this love all exercise of spiritual gifts is worthless.

We believe Jesus Christ is the head of the Body, His church, and that church government should be simplistic rather than a complex beauracracy. We desire to be led by the Holy Spirit in all the functions and directions of the ministry of the church.

We await the pre-tribulational rapture of the church, and we believe that the second coming of Christ with His saints to rule on the earth will be personal pre-millennial, and visible. This motivates us to holy living, heartfelt worship, committed service, diligent study of God's Word, regular fellowship, and participation in baptism by immersion and in Holy Communion.

We seek to teach the Word of God in such a way that its message can be applied to an individual's life, leading that person to greater maturity in Christ.

We reject doctrinal viewpoints or spiritual phenomena which are based solely on experience. We look to the Word of God for the basis of all our faith and practice.

We believe that the nation of Israel has a special place in God's plan and that all the promises of God to Israel will be fulfilled.

035. Statement Of Faith

We believe the Bible to be the inspired and only infallible Word of God.

We believe that there is one God eternally existent in three persons: God the Father, God the Son, and God the Holy Spirit.

We believe in the blessed hope, which is the rapture of the Church of God which is in Christ in His return.

We believe that the only means of being cleansed from sin is through repentance, faith in the precious blood of Jesus Christ, and belief in the gospel according to Romans 10:9-10.

We believe that regeneration by the Holy Ghost is absolutely essential for personal salvation.

We believe that the redemptive work of Christ on the cross provides healing for the human body in answer to believing prayer.

We believe that the baptism in the Holy Ghost, according to Acts 2:4 is given to believers who ask for it.

We believe in the sanctifying power of the Holy Spirit by whose indwelling the Christian is enabled to live a holy and separated life in this present world. Amen.

036. Statement Of Faith

(1) We believe that Scripture is the infallible record of God's historic self-revelation to man. It is without error in its original writings. It is also the means by which God continually speaks to His children, calling them to faithful obedience and instructing them in Christian growth.

(2) We believe that God is one in essence, yet exists eternally in three co-equal persons: Father, Son, Holy Spirit. He has revealed Himself to be perfect in love, righteous in all His ways and Creator of all things.
(3) We believe that every member of the human race is a sinner by nature and deed.
(4) We believe that Jesus Christ is God manifest in the flesh, born of a virgin, sinless, crucified for our sins, resurrected from the dead, ascended to heaven and coming back again to establish His kingdom on earth.
(5) We believe that people become children of God when they repent of their sin and trust in Jesus Christ alone as Lord and Savior.
(6) We believe that the Holy Spirit indwells the life of the believer providing strength and wisdom for loving and living according to the will of God.
(7) We believe the Church is the living Body of Christ on earth. He is its head and the source of its life. The Body is composed of those who have received Him as Savior and Lord.
(8) We believe that a true believer is eternally secure, that he cannot lose his salvation, but sin may interrupt the joy of his fellowship with God and bring loving discipline from his Heavenly Father.
(9) We believe Jesus Christ will return to the earth to raise the dead, judge the world and establish His glorious Kingdom This is the hope of the Church and its encouragement for ministry. Those who do not believe in Him will receive eternal punishment and separation from God.

037. Statement Of Faith

(1) We believe the Bible to be the inspired, the only infallible, authoritative Word of God.
(2) We believe that there is one God eternally existent in three persons: Father, Son and Holy Spirit.
(3) We believe in the Deity of our Lord Jesus Christ, in His virgin birth, in His sinless life, in His miracles, in His vicarious atoning death through His shed blood, in His bodily resurrection, in His ascension to the right hand of the Father and in His personal return in power and glory.
(4) We believe that for the salvation of lost and sinful man regeneration by the Holy Spirit is absolutely essential.
(5) We believe in the present ministry of the Holy Spirit by whose indwelling the Christian is enabled to live a godly life.

(6) We believe in the resurrection of both the saved and the lost; they that are saved unto the resurrection of life and they that are lost unto the resurrection of damnation.

(7) We believe in the spiritual unity of believers in our Lord Jesus Christ.

038. Statement Of Faith

We Believe the Bible to be the inspired and only infallible Word of God. We believe that there is one God eternally existent in Three Persons, God the Father, God the Son, God the Holy Spirit.

We Believe in the blessed hope, which is in the rapture of the Church of God which is in Christ at His return.

We Believe that the only means of being cleansed from sin is through repentance, faith in the precious Blood of Jesus Christ and being baptized in water. We believe that regeneration by the Holy Ghost is absolutely essential for personal salvation.

We Believe that the redemptive work of Christ on the cross provides healing for the human body in answer to believing prayer.

We Believe that the baptism in the Holy Ghost, according to Acts 2:4 is given to believers who ask for it.

We Believe in the sanctifying power of the Holy Spirit by whose indwelling the Christian is enabled to live a holy and separated life in this present world. Amen.

CHAPTER 3

Mission Statements

A mission statement is concerned with a goal, the purpose of which is to clarify the aim of the church and unify the congregation.

Mission statements begin with "To be...," "To become...," "To build...," "To bring...," "To develop...," "To discover...," "To exalt...," "To help...," "To serve...," etc.

Occasionally a mission statement needs to be reviewed or rewritten to help unify the congregation. Beside mission statements, churches should have stated goals in the areas of worship attendance, stewardship, evangelism, and community outreach, limiting the number of goals to the time, effort, and expenses needed to accomplish them. Also, determine how many goals the church can handle and the order of priority.

Listed in this chapteer are 50 mission statements; and in the appendix are 264 mission slogans.

Mission Statements

039. To Administer God's Love by
Proclaiming a relevant gospel
Learning to serve God by serving others
Activating new members
Creating opportunities for everyone
Engaging time, talent, and resources God's way

040. To advance the Gospel locally and internationally, by actions and words, boldly and confidently, in the power of the Spirit. We are committed to building faithful and devoted followers of Christ, walking in holiness, love and unity, reflecting the beauty of the Gospel in all their responsibilities and relationships.

041. To advance the Kingdom of God, and to participate in events whose focus is healing and uniting the Body of Christ, always striving to produce quality service in representing Christ in the highest aspect.

042. To advance the Kingdom of the Lord Jesus Christ in the world through local outreach, campus ministry, world missions, and church planting. We are making disciples, training leaders, and reaching youth.

043. To assure that worship glorifies God, inspires the people who gather for worship, and encourages the people to develop their individual and shared witness to Christ.

044. To assemble together to glorify God in Worship, to be devoted to prayer and to God's Word, to challenge and edify believers in Jesus Christ to become disciples, and to evangelize our community and the world through our words and actions.

045. To be an authentic expression of the Kingdom of God by
- declaring the reconciling love of God in Christ,
- modeling that love in the quality of our living,
- preparing all who respond to that love to become fully devoted followers of Christ
- living toward a community identified by inclusive relationships and accepting grace

046. To be a contemporary Christian witness in our community, celebrating the continuing presence and power of our loving God, redeeming Christ, and sustaining Spirit. We seek to be a place of personal and spiritual growth for all, a place where we are nurtured and challenged in our faith and lives. We strive to be a caring, healing, and renewing fellowship open to the rich diversity of our community. We commit ourselves to continue reaching out to our community and the world with love and compassion, always praying and working for justice and peace.

047. To be a growing church that is spiritually alive to God and actively caring for others. This vision sets us on a journey, calling us to worship Jesus Christ as Lord and Savior, to respond to the needs of people through caring ministries of healing and hope, to celebrate our diversity of prospective while affirming our unity in Christ, and, through the Holy Spirit, to grow in our discovery of God and our mission in the world. We pursue this vision with creativity and imagination, enjoying laughter, extending compassion, all to make God's love relevant and fresh.

048. To be a local expression of the **"Bride of Christ": W**orship, **I**nstruction, **F**ellowship, **E**vangelism.

049. To be a model of the Lord Jesus Christ by keeping His commandments and fulfilling His commission. **Definitions: Vision:** (for ministry) is a clear mental image of a preferable future imparted by God to His chosen servants and is based upon an accurate understanding of God, self, and circumstances. **Model:** is to demonstrate by experience how something or someone works. **Keeping:** is to obey or use as a guideline for obedience. His commandments:

> *And Jesus came and spoke to them, saying, "All authority has been given to Me in heaven and on earth. Go, therefore, and make disciples of all nations, baptizing them in the name of the Father and of the Son and of the Holy Spirit, teaching them to observe all things that I have commanded you; and lo, I am with you always, even to the end of the age.* Amen. Matthew 22:37-40

050. To be a community of believers united by faith, Scripture, and the constitution of our denomination committed to calling people to Christ and encouraging one another in faith through worship, education, fellowship and service.

051. To be a "Reaching Out and Inviting" Church that Shares God's Love and Models Jesus Christ To the Next Generation.

Exaltation—We gather together in worship and prayer to exalt God and delight in Him.

Edification—We commit to small group ministry to mature in love for each other and God.

Education—We participate in educational training to grow in the knowledge of our faith.

Evangelism—We reach out in love to unchurched people to make new followers of Jesus.

052. To be empowered by our Baptism, to make Christ present through our proclamation of the Gospel, our celebration of the Sacraments, and our service to one another, especially those most in need. Being inclusive and rich in diversity of age, ethnicity, gifts, and way of life—to provide a place of challenge and opportunity for growth in order that we might act justly, individually and as a community, in building the Reign of God.

053. To be *"the light of the world"* (Matthew 5:14) by presenting Jesus Christ in creative, credible, and caring ways to all people and by providing an environment that encourages them to grow to their full potential in Christ.

054. To be empowered by God, helping people in our area become like Christ through worship, Christian education, fellowship, outreach, and ministries.

055. To be

Joyful in Song,
Earnest in the Holy Spirit,
Satisfying to the Soul,
Uplifting His name,
Salvation for the Lost and Strength for the Saints

056. To become a prayerful, loving, multi-ethnic, and dynamic Christian people who practice transformational ministry that reconciles people with the living God.

057. To become all that God desires us to be. We worship the Lord, share the Good News wherever we are, both in our lifestyles and through our words, educate and prepare God's people for ministry, and encourage each other to maturing in Christ.

058. To become a prayerful, loving, multi-ethnic and dynamic Christian people in our area who practice transformational ministry that reconciles people with the the living God.

059. To bring an ever increasing number of people into an ever closer relationship with Jesus Christ so that God's love may be a transforming force for the communities in which we live.

060. To build a community of faithful believers who are committed to reaching up, reaching in, and reaching out.

061. To build and nurture Christian disciples through worship, study, prayer, and service. Affirming each person's unique gifts and talents we invite others into a loving, prayerful relationship with God. As the scattered church of Jesus Christ, we are sent forth into the world to service and to challenge injustice.

062. To bring people to Jesus as a MEMBER of His family, to develop them to Christ-like MATURITY, to equip them for MINISTRY in the church and life MISSION in the world in order to MAGNIFY the name of the Lord. **Strategy:**

1. Bring them: **Evangelism**
2. Build them up: **Worship, Fellowship, Discipleship**
3. Train them for service: **Ministry**
4. Send them out: **Evangelism**

063. To build a church where every person, no matter where they are on their spiritual journey, can experience the peace, power, healing and grace of God--through Jesus Christ.

064. To build a church where we are Challenged toward maturity in our spiritual lives, genuinely Care for each other, Communicate Christ to those who need His salvation, and Celebrate the glory of our God.

065. To

Celebrate through worship,
Heed the Word,
Respond in loving service to others,
Invite others to our family,
Serve the Lord with all our heart,
Teach all people about salvation through Christ.

066. To bring people to Jesus; to help mature and equip followers of Jesus to ministerto the body, as well as to individually reach out to the lost, hurting, and disadvantaged surrounding us; to encourage and maintain a loving community of those who gather here; to aim toward being a full service ministry, providing as complete an offering to all ages and interests as possible within the scope of our God-given fiscal resources. To be a ministry that demonstrates we are willing to walk by faith and not by sight alone—striking the balance that fits God's heart for us; thoughtfully and prayerfully staff our ministry with capable pastors and lay people who will work with each other to accomplish the job we believe God has put before us.

Regardless of what we may do, we shall be mindful that our primary calling as an assembly is to engage in meaningful and heartfelt worship that celebrates and glorifies God.

067. To build a healthy and celebrating church family attractive to a postmodern generation of seekers, helping everyone mature to become whole people and devoted Christ-followers.

068. To Continue the work of Jesus, peacefully, simply, together—
Builder and Owner: Jesus Christ. Matt. 16:18
Qualified leadership: Elders and Deacons. Titus 1:5-9
Doctrine: The Bible only
Members: Christians.

069. To cooperate with God by giving Him glory through inspiring Worship Services that draw both Christians and non-Christians into His immediate presence and facilitate an atmosphere of obedient, passionate and Spirit-led worship.

070. To (1) Communicate God's Word, (2) Celebrate God's Presence, (3) Assimilate God's Family, (4) Educate God's People, (5) Demonstrate God's Love

071. To be **Called** to a ministry of grace, passionate about Christ's mission in the world through: **Worship**, centering the church in a shared encounter with merciful God: Father, Son, and Holy Spirit; **Nurture** in the Word of God, equipping Christians of all ages to serve as Christ's light in the world; a **Community** of committed servants, in which everyone receives care when in need and offers care when able; and **Outreach**, engaging the world through every member who serves as a missionary of God's love.

072. To CELEBRATE Christ, to CULTIVATE personal growth in Christ, to CARE for one another in Christ, to COMMUNICATE Christ in our community and world.

073. To come together to Celebrate Grace, Grow in Understanding, Support and be Supported, Honor Diversity, Respond to a World in Crisis.

074. To come together by the Holy Spirit for the specific purpose of preaching and teaching the Word of God (the Bible), and about Jesus Christ, God's Son, and to proclaim the gospel of the kingdom of God to our community and its environs; To be a center of genuine concern for those in need, a sanctuary of community worship that is neither shallow nor restrained, a spiritual home where members find an expression of precious love for one another and a haven for the unsaved.

075. To cultivate a spirit of praise and worship at (name of church). We aim to help believers recognize their identity as a *"chosen people, a royal priesthood, a holy nation, a people belonging to God, that [we] may declare the praises of Him Who called [us] out of darkness into His wonderful light."* I Peter 2:9-10

076. To develop a Biblical functioning community that impacts our surrounding community with the life-changing truth of Jesus Christ.

077. To develop committed followers of Jesus Christ as we **EXALT** God with our worship; **EXAMINE** and apply God's Word; **EMPHASIZE** prayer; **EXPRESS** our spiritual gifts; **EXTEND** God's love in outreach.

078. To empower people with an awareness of their own spiritual nature as taught and demonstrated by Jesus Christ in an atmosphere of nonjudgmental love.

079. To engage people locally and internationally by the Holy Spirit through word and deed with the gospel of Jesus Christ for the sake of God's Kingdom.

080. To evangelize the world, to edify the body, to mobilize our people, to win others for Christ, to incorporate them into the fellowship of the church.

081. To **Exalt** and worship the Lord our God and Jesus Christ our Savior expanding membership in God's family along with **Educating** them for spiritual maturity; **Equipping** them for ministry and seeking together to **Evangelize** the world.

082. To exalt Jesus Christ and to make Him and His Spirit visible to our community and to the whole world by empowering, disciplining, and releasing God's people the Body of Christ into their God-given ministries. We seek to reflect the character of Christ through His body, the Church, so that everyone we touch may hear and encounter His message. We will do this through our five-fold focus of **EXALTING** the Lord, **ENTERING** into prayer, **EDIFYING** the body, **EVANGELIZING** the lost, and **EMBRACING** the needs of others.

083. To discover how Jesus' challenge to "love one another" can be lived out today in our world. We live in a world often divided by race and nationality, and so we affirm the diverse ways the Gospel comes alive in our multi-cultural parish community. We live in a world where many of us are hungry for spiritual nourishment, and so we gather to hear the Word of God and to celebrate community at the Lord's table. We live in a world where many of us do not appreciate our unique value in God's eyes, and so we strive to be welcoming, nurturing and hospitable in all our gatherings in order that all of us may recognize our importance in the community. We live in a world where there are poor, hungry, homeless people, both within and outside of our parish borders, and so we try in many ways to reach out and continue Jesus' ministry of "going about and doing good" so that all may experience the Kingdom of God through us.

084. To discover that we get the most out of life when we are actively involved in our relationship with Christ Jesus. Our goal is to provide an involvement opportunity that is just right for you. We invite you to discover a special place for you here.

085. To Empower Leadership—We will equip, support, motivate, and mentor an expanding core of ministry leaders in the dynamics of spiritual leadership so that a broader base of lay people are engaged in turning God's vision for their lives.... **Passionate Spirituality**—We will become a people more passionate about developing a heart like Jesus.... **Need-Orientated Evangelism**—We will educate and motivate the entire body of our membership to develop a lifestyle of compassion and generosity that leads to sharing the Gospel in a way that meets the questions and needs of non-Christians whom we know.

086. To embrace diversity and individual conscience, while celebrating spirituality in our community; to strive to do justly, to love mercy, to move humble in harmony with all creation. We affirm devotion to spirit, service others, and the life of the mind and body. We are a sanctuary for the troubled spirit, mind, and body. We are a people of all ages, races, colors, cultures, origins and abilities.

087. To **EVANGELIZE** the lost; **ENCOURAGE** the lost to come to Christ and grow in Him; **EQUIP** believers to serve the body and win the lost. **EXALT** the Lord Jesus Christ in our services and in our individual lives.

088. To Exalt God through corporate worship; **Equip the believe**r through teaching and preaching, to **Extend into our community** through our fellowship and outreach; and by these things **become what God has intended us to be:** His people, complete in Christ, lacking nothing.

089. To extend the Gospel internationally working in and through local church ministries, to strengthen churches through leadership training, seminars, and conferences; to provide literature, equipment, and support to missionaries and national pastors and workers, to encourage interest and support for missions through teaching, seminars, conferences, and literature.

090. To gather faithfully in worship of God Who gives us life, to translate the words of faith into acts of compassion and mercy. to give ourselves to each other in Christ-like love, to serve the Lord and reflect His majesty, power, and love.

091. To glorify God, to encourage a commitment to Jesus Christ as Savior and Lord and to equip the believers for works of service here and abroad.

092. To glorify God through worshipping, witnessing, nurturing, equipping, and sending faithful, loving, and obedient followers of Jesus Christ here and to the ends of the earth.

093. To help fulfill the Great Commission—not just in our community, but to all nations. This Commission challenges us to make disciples among all nations, to baptize them and to teach them to live under the Lordship of Jesus Christ. Matt. 28:19-20

094. To grow spiritually in our relationship with God, having fellowship with one another, and extending ourselves to those in need. To share the Gospel enabling people to have meaningful and life-changing relationships with Jesus Christ so they can be healed and empowered. To celebrate the love of God by strengthening the Church as the body of Christ, cultivating the diverse spiritual gifts of all our members.

095. To help our members grow in their worship of God, understand the Bible, and show God's love in church and family life so that they may share their faith and hope in Jesus Christ...to inform, inspire, and equip leaders...to provide training, encouragement, and counsel...and to make available a variety of special ministries.

096. To glorify God by reaching out to our community and to the world with Christ's love. We fulfill this purpose by:

Glorifying
- by praising God in all things,
- by expressing God's love with our lives,
- by being obedient and faithful in His service.

Reaching
- by reaching out to people in our community with the good news of Jesus Christ,
- by reaching out to help those in our community who are in need,
- by accepting God's will for our life with joy.

Accepting
- by accepting one another as Jesus Christ accepts us,
- by accepting ourselves as loved and valued by God,
- by accepting God's will for our life with joy.

Celebrating
- by celebrating our unity in Christ,
- by gathering together to worship God actively and joyfully,
- by celebrating God's Grace, showing joy in our personal lives.

Educating
- by maintaining a Biblical foundation for our teaching,
- by developing spiritual maturity at all levels by practical application of Biblical truth,
- by equipping people for ministry through helping them discover and develop their unique skills.
- by nurturing youth in personal and spiritual growth.

097. To let the Bible shape our faith: *"All Scripture is God-breathed and is useful for teaching, rebuking, correcting and training in righteousness, so that the man of God may be thoroughly equipped for every good work."* **2 Timothy 3:16-17**

To pray to our Father regularly: *"Do not be anxious about anything, but in prayer and petition, with thanksgiving, present your requests to God."* **Philippians 4:6**

To gather weekly for worship: *"Come, let us bow down in worship, let us kneel before the Lord our Maker; for He is our God, and we are the people of His pasture, the flock under His care."* **Psalm 95:6,7**

To warmly welcome people "in process": *"Accept one another, just as Christ accepted you in order to praise to God."* **Romans 15:7**

To model Jesus' love in our relationships: *"A new command I give you: Love one another. As I have loved you, so you must love one another. By this will all men will know that you are my disciples, if you love one another."* **John 13:34-35**

To meet in small groups for spiritual growth: *"Every day they continued to meet together in the temple courts. They broke bread in their homes and ate together with glad and sincere hearts."* **Acts 2: 46**

To develop our members into ministers: *"Each one using whatever gift he has received to faithfully minister God's grace in its many forms."* **I Peter 4:10**

To honor the Lord's commitment to our children: *"I will establish my covenant between me and you and your descendants after you for generations to come, to be our God and the God of your descendants after you."* **Genesis 17:7**

To place our resources under God's management: *"Therefore, I urge you, brothers, in view of God's mercy, to offer your bodies as living sacrifices, holy and pleasing to God; this is our spiritual act of worship."* **Romans 12:1**

To bring our ministry into our community: *"He has committed to us the message of reconciliation. therefore we are Christ's ambassadors, as though God were making His appeal through us. We implore you on Christ's behalf: be reconciled to God."* **2 Corinthians 5:20**

098. To joyfully worship God by leading people to Christ's family, ensuring Christian growth, and equipping all for outreach and service.

099. To love and worship God; to encourage, love and care; to minister to every believer; to faithfully preach God's Word; to teach Biblical truth; to pray without ceasing; to joyfully give thanks to the Father.

100. To live out our purpose through
Service: by providing practical services for and in support of the members and of our church and community.
Worship: by affirming the Eucharist as the primary action of worship in our life together.
Evangelism: by proclaiming by word and example the Good News in Jesus Christ through the power of the Holy Spirit.
Education: by equipping the saints to do the mission of the church.
Pastoral Care: by providing opportunities for pastoral care and spiritual direction to every parishioner and friend.
Stewardship: by upholding the scriptural principles of the offering in money, time, and talent.

101. To nurture one another in relationships with Jesus Christ; to reach out so others may experience God's love through us; to equip one another for serving here and everywhere; to worship the Lord and enjoy Him forever.

102. To obey God gratefully. Following Scripture we strive to glorify God by loving Him with all our being, loving our neighbors as ourselves, and sharing the love and good news of Jesus Christ. By praying and depending on the Holy Spirit we seek to be Christ's faithful witnesses.

103. To offer and encourage Christian caring, and competent service to the church community with education, enrichment, prevention, support, and repair. To provide a context of healing and hope with concern for the whole person and focus on the emotional and relational wellness needs.

104. To offer the body of believers the opportunity to worship and glorify God together, to build up the Body of Christ through God's Word, to affect change in the lives of believers, to encourage people to become participating members and develop meaningful relationships, to pray together fervently for the plans and purposes of God to be accomplished in the earth, to reach people who are facing a Christless eternity.

105. To present ourselves to God in spirit and truth, as He transforms our lives **(A worshipping Congregation);** to love sinful people toward spiritual, personal and relational wholeness **(A Healing Community);** to deepen scriptural knowledge, discover spiritual gifts, and deploy individuals in service **(An Equipping Center);** to make disciples as God's witnesses in our community, nation, and throughout the world.

106. To
Proclaim the Gospel of Jesus Christ (Mark:16:15), to
Assist the hurting and needy with love and benevolence (James 1:27), to
Revere, praise, worship, and love the almighty and living God (Psalm 150), to
Kindle a spiritual awakening in our area by prayer and actions (II Cron. 7:14), to
Win people to Jesus Christ by all means possible (I Cor. 9:25b), to
Arm the saints for an effective ministry (Eph. 4:11-13), to
Yield the fruit of the Holy Spirit.
(Parkway Baptist Church)

107. To provide an atmosphere that is Friendly and Accepting; To Welcome Guests; To Show God's Love; To Help Each Person Feel Part of the Friendly Atmosphere.

108. To provide a fellowship where single adults can and will be challenged to experience the grace of God in their lives. God's grace and mercy empowers us to love God and others, resulting in exciting growth and change. We invite everyone, regardless of the life situation, to come and experience God's grace!

109. To reach out to the lost and unchurched people with the Gospel within the sphere of our influence in a sensitive and relevant way. To offer a ministry that is characterized by a loving, healing, faith-filled environment where everyone can grow to the full potential in Christ.

110. To reach out to lost and unchurched people with the gospel within the sphere of our influence in a sensitive and relevant way. We offer a ministry that is characterized by a loving, healing, faith-filled environment where everyone can grow to their full potential in Christ.

110. To serve our immediate parish community by implementing the Great Commission in Matthew 28:18-20 and ministering to the needs of God's people (Matthew 25:34-40). **In order to accomplish this we will:** Aggressively reach into our community using all forms of communication available to tell the story of Jesus Christ.... Actively recruit new members who will be committed to Jesus Christ.... Educate children and adults in the basic truths of the Bible and how to live a Christian life.... Identify the diverse physical and spiritual needs of the congregation and community and respond as we have talent, resources, and abilities.... Provide an uplifting worship experience.

112. To serve our Lord Jesus Christ and to glorify Him through our worship and ministry. Our aim is to share the good news of eternal life through Jesus Jesus Christ in our community through faithful evangelism, and to the world through our missionary endeavor. Our ministry to our church family is to assist them in growing in their personal faith and to equip them to serve the Lord in their personal ministries. Our worship to God endeavors to be dynamic by excelling in spirit and truth. Our foundation is built on the principles of God's Word which is our authority in life and practice.

113. To serve the living God by developing a loving, committed Christian community through:

- vibrant, relevant and Bible-based worship
- Spirit-empowered and whole-person evangelism
- comprehensive Christian nurture
- equipping for joyful service
- fostering Christian community

114. To support individuals in experiencing conscious awareness of God. Our mission is to create a sanctuary where we as individuals can realize God in our lives and model, teach, call forth, and celebrate the integrity of spirit, mind, and body in all that we do.

115. To worship God faithfully together, to be people in Christ, and by the grace of the Holy Spirit, to do God's work in this place. As a community of faith committed to healing and wholeness we carry out this mission through worship, preaching, teaching, and nurturing community life. Our goal is to follow the Savior by practicing acceptance, inclusiveness, love, justice, and peace.

CHAPTER 4

Church Facilities

This chapter deals with the church grounds and buildings, especially the parking lot and sanctuary. The larger the parking lot, the more attention to details is needed. Some churches have attendants on the lot with hand-held radios. One church had a space for motorcycles.

In the sanctuary make sure the American flag and the Christian flag are properly placed. The American flag is on the speaker's right as he/she faces the audience, or on the audience's left, facing the speaker.

Look at your facilities from the eyes of a visitor and try to determine what message your facilities are communicating. Two most important areas are the nursery and the restrooms.

Church Facilities

Parking

116. Have spaces for **"FIRST TIME VISITORS"** as well as **"VISITORS."**

117. Have spaces for **"ADULT SENIORS"** or **"SENIOR SAINTS."**

118. If the parking lot is large, have spaces numbered for easy location after church.

119. Have parking space labeled, **"CLERGY SPACE: YOU PARK, YOU PREACH."**

120. Have space reserved for the_______________family.

121. Have a sign for Church Staff Parking, **"VIOLATERS WILL BE BAPTIZED."**

122. Have sign, **"NO PARKING! VIOLATORS WILL BE TURNED INTO A PILLAR OF SALT."**

123. In larger churches have reserved spaces in parking lot for single ladies attending the evening services.

124. On the street in front of the church, have a sign, **"NEW VISITORS PARKING."**

125. Have a sign at the front of church or entrance to parking lot, **"VALET PARKING AVAILABLE."**

126. Have all church workers and other volunteers to park in the back, leaving closer spaces to others.

127. Have a sign on church grounds, **"THESE PREMISES AND PARKING LOTS ARE MONITORED BY VIDEO SURVELANCE."**

128. Have a Welcome Committee in the parking lot.

129. Have a large sign at parking lot exit, **"NOW THE SERVICE BEGINS."**

130. Have an Umbrella Ministry from the street to the front door of the church to keep worshippers out of the rain.

In the Sanctuary

131. Instead of stained glass windows, if there is scenery or trees, or mountains have large clear glass windows.

132. Have a small booklet on the symbolism and meaning of stained glass windows, listing dedication dates and names of donors, and names of persons in whose memory the windows have been dedicated.

133. Have a workshop on paper cutting tapestries, large scale designs for worship services. Church members are taught how to create designs from the Creation to the Rapture. Contact Alice Helen Masek, 2520 Craig Ct., Castro Valley, CA 94546. Phone 510-538-2617; E-mail alicehelen@juno.com.

134. Have hanging lamp shades with crosses on them.

135. Have designated pews with earphones for the hearing impaired.

136. Have sign on last pew "Reserved For Parents With Small Children"

137. Have church business cards in pew racks with maps of church or direction to the church on the back.

138. Have one person responsible for the pew racks, pencils, envelopes, cards.

139. Have cushions on end of pews.

140. Have tissues on end of pews.

141. Have children's distress notification—number displays on small screen in the upper front of the sanctuary for parents to report to the nursery if needed.

142. If the pulpit/lectern is open or glass or plastic, put flowers or plants in front.

143. Place a large open Bible in front of the pulpit.

144. Have a plaque on the pulpit, **"Pastor, do you love us?"**

145. Have a plaque on the pulpit, **"Sir, we would see Jesus."**

146. Have pads in front by rail for worshippers to go forward, kneel, and pray.

147. Have overhead projector screen hymns, Scripture, announcements, visitors' welcome, points in pastor's sermon, and words to solos or other special musicals.

148. Change the background of the screen from white to black or use color filter with white lighted cross.

149. Have screen in back for choir and leader to see.

150. Have a recycling bin for bulletins.

151. Have a plaque over the drinking fountain, ***"Whosoever drinks of this water shall thirst again, but whosoever drinks of the water that I shall give him shall never thirst."***

152. Have a full-length mirror in the ladies room.

153. Have a memorial garden—a meditation center to provide a meaningful place for the internment of the ashes of the departed.

154. Have special bench in front of auditorium with plaque, **"In loving memory of ________________(name and date)"**

155. Have a large replica of a butterfly near the cross signifying the resurrection.

156. Have a welcome sign for visitors in the foyer.

157. Have a members' name tag rack with tags to be picked up before going into the service, to be returned after the service.

158. Have a "Blessing Box" or "Blessing Basket" with different blessings on slips of paper, rolled with rubber band. Worshippers pick out a blessing before entering the sanctuary. Example of blessing, *"I treat everyone I meet with courtesy and respect."* (No swapping or trading).

159. Have a banner with the church mission slogan on it.

160. Have a "Preachers Hall of Fame" listing members of the church who have gone into full-time Christian service.

161. In the foyer have pictures of church leaders and/or church staff.

162. Have a framed board with names and pictures of new members.

163. Have pictures of missionaries the church supports with short summary of their work. Have a light button connected to a large map showing their country.

164. Have photo pictures of any subject taken by members displayed with corresponding Scripture. Then have members vote on (1) best photo, (2) best interconnection.

165. Have a sign over the doorway to the church, "ENTER WITH THANKSGIVING AND PRAISE."

166. Have a note on the main door to sanctuary. "Please enter side door after the service begins."

167. In the sanctuary or foyer have flags displayed of all countries in which missions or missionaries are supported.

168. Have loudspeaker in foyer or outside with music and worship service.

CHAPTER 5
Membership

It Is interesting to find out how different churches deal with membership. Some churches have covenants to which prospective members are pledged to keep. Membership classes are required as is testimony before the church board and/or membership. One church with thousands of members accepted members without question—just a hand shake.

Whatever the conditions of membership are should be in print and available to prospective members. The goal of the membership process is not only making decisions, but also making disciples. In smaller churches where the pastor does most of the visitation and member recruitment , he/she should not stop visiting the new members but try to get them involved in the church program.

Most churches visited had new members' classes, sometimes called "Pastor's Class," "Inquirer's Class," or "Orientation Class".

This chapter deals with membership provisions, preparation, and procedures.

MEMBERSHIP

Provisions

169. The membership is composed of those who have accepted the Lord Jesus Christ as their personal Savior and are willing to leave minor points of doctrine to the direction of the Holy Spirit upon the individual's conscience. Everyone who unites with the church states by doing so that he or she is volunteering for active service. Those desiring to make this their home may contact the pastor at_______________.

170. Membership in the church is open to those who, through faith in the Son of God, our Lord Jesus Christ, have been born again to a living hope; by faith in Jesus Christ, have manifested themselves as true Christians as defined in the Holy Scripture; have been baptized according to the Holy Scriptures, and desire to join in the ministry of the church and to share its fellowship and obligations.

171. Our membership is open to all individuals who have received Jesus Christ as Savior and Lord and have obeyed His command to be baptized by immersion. This is possible by an initial expression of desire for membership or by transfer from another church.

Steps to Membership:

a. Present yourself for membership by coming forward during the invitation at the close of a service.
b. A counselor will meet with you.
c. The counselor will arrange to meet with you at a convenient time during the week.
d. You will attend the Membership Class.
e. You will give your testimony before the Board of Deacons.
f. Upon approval by the Board of Deacons, you will be presented for membership acceptance in the evening service on the first Sunday of the month.

172. It is our desire that each person seeking membership receive a full overview of our church. To achieve this, we offer the **Inquirer's Class** three times a year. This class is for those wishing to become members, as well as for those who are simply interested in learning more about Christ and the Church.

173. Our church extends an invitation to membership to any person who is ready to commit to the joys and challenges of being part of a community of faith. Persons from all denominational backgrounds and persons with no previous church affiliation are always welcome. Individuals who join the church are asked to support the church with their prayers, presence, gifts, and service. Taking these vows of membership is often the first step in a more deliberate relationship with God, a more fulfilling spiritual life, and more meaningful spiritual life, and more meaningful involvement in the church. However, not everyone is ready to make the commitment to church membership. Regardless of whether or not you become a member, you are welcome to worship with us and participate in our ministries. We invite you to journey alongside us as you explore ways to develop and nurture yourself and serve God through this community of faith.

174. COVENANT OF MEMBERSHIP—Having personally received Jesus Christ as Savior and Lord, and having considered favorably the Biblical doctrines and practices of (name of) Church, and being in agreement with the tenets of faith, and desiring to be associated with those of like precious faith in Christian fellowship, I hereby apply for membership in the body of (name of) Church.

I agree to submit myself to the statutes and standards of Biblical conduct, and subsequently, commit to support the church with prayer, faithful attendance, as well as tithes and offerings as God shall prosper.

It is my earnest prayer that God will keep me true to Him, but if for any reason I depart from the faith or cease to live a godly life, I shall consider it just cause to be released from membership.

Preparing for Membership

175. Have group discussion by members to discuss the reasons for getting new members.

176. Assign a "fellowship friend" to each new member to keep in contact for three to six months.

177. Have membership policy printed in bulletin.

178. Have membership seminar all Sunday afternoon instead of stretching it out over a period of weeks.

179. Membership orientation class required to become a member, covering doctrine, history and organization of the church. However, attending the class does not obligate one to join the church.

180. Have new members fill out an interest indicator form.

181. Our church does not accept transfer membership. All must go through orientation and give their testimony.

Procedures

182. Have new membership class soon after joining.

183. Interview new members to see what their interests and talents are. Then match their gifts to the needs of the church.

184. Have new members listed in bulletin. They come forward for the official welcome. Pastor introduces each one and prays for them.

185. Have the pictures of new members in the foyer.

186. The pastor or deacon presents new members with a certificate of membership.

187. Have a short biography of each new member in the bulletin/ insert.

188. On first Sunday list names and addresses of new members of the previous month.

189. Select one or two members from the congregation to come forward and greet new members on behalf of the church..

190. During the service new members are called by name to come to the front. Pastor introduces them to the congregation and says a few words about each, prays for each, then gives certificates of membership. Members then go down one side and give the new members the right hand of fellowship.

191. As the offering is brought forward, the new members go to the front where the minister has offertory prayer, then receives the new members.

192. New members, or candidates for membership, go forward during the worship service. Pastor introduces them to the congregation, then asks them as a group regarding their faith, missions, etc. at which they say "I do." Pastor gives the right hand of fellowship and certificate of membership then has the members in the congregation pledge their prayers and support and encouragement.

193. Give new members a candle and some clay to be molded in any shape of their choosing for the base of the candle. Ask them what the light stands for (prepare them in advance for this question).

194. Have new members come forward to have their pictures taken to be placed in the narthex/foyer.

CHAPTER 6
Children and Youth Ministries

Churches that have strong children's and youth's programs have a bright future. Those that do not will die. Fifty years ago I attended a large church with a seating capacity of several hundred. Every Sunday morning the church was filled because, among other things, they had a strong youth program. Recently I visited that same church. The youth program was gone and I don't think they even had Sunday School. At the Sunday morning worship service there were 35 (counting myself); and the average age was in the 80's. Where will that church be ten years from now—or even five?

This chapter covers the young people from nursery age to high school and college. There is a wide selection of names for various groups.

Children and Youth Ministries

195. Names of nursery groups
  a. Angels' Academy
  b. Happy Time Nursery School
  c. Joyful Noise Nursery
  d. Tiny Treasurers
  e. Tots and Toddlers
  f. Wee Adventurers
  g. Wee Kids

196. Train all ushers and greeters to answer questions about the nursery.

197. Invite all pre-school and kindergarten children to participate in the worship service until the end of the children's sermon

198. Hire non-Christians for nursery workers (to reach them for Christ).

199. Have security checks for all nursery workers and train them.

200. Assign each parent a number which in case of emergency is shown on a small screen in the sanctuary.

201. Give a beeper to an usher or greeter for emergencies.

202. Have a high standard of cleanliness. Sterilize toys before they are used. Have the sheets and blankets washed after use by each child. Sterilize the diaper changing table after each use.

203. Have a cry room for mothers who wish to nurse their babies.

204. Have a "Comfort Room" for parents with infants. Have sound-proof glass so they can watch the service, and speakers so they can hear.

205. If children stay for the worship service, sit in the front rows with an adult. Children who can see will feel a part of the worship service.

206. During the Peace, greet children as well as their parents.

207. Hand offering plates to children, not over their heads.

208. Ensure children have a bulletin of their own.

Sunday School

209. Other names for Sunday School
a. Christian Education Classes
b. Christian Education Hour
c. Christian Life Hour
d. Discovery Hour
e. Discovery Classes
f. Education Focus
g. Exploring the Bible Hour
h. Religious Education
i. Sunday Study Hour

211. Names for lower grades
a. Adventure Club
b. Boys' Brigade
c. Buck-A-Roos (boys)
d. Christian Service Brigade
e. Cornerstone Kids
f. Confident Kids
g. Glory Girls
h. God Squad
i. Good News Kids' Club
j. Jesus and Me
k. Joy Club
l. Kangaroos
m. Kids' Company
n. Kids' Klub
o. Kids' Patch (children living with one parent)
p. Kidsville
q. Kids Under Construction
r. Kids' Zone
s. Koolas
t. Missionettes (girls)
u. Otters
v. Pioneer Girls
w. Raccoons
x. Rainbow Kids
y. Royal Rangers (boys)
z. Shining Lights
aa. Straight Arrows (boys)
bb. Trailblazers (boys)
cc. Windjammers (boys)

210. Names for pre-school
a. Cubbies
b. GloWorms
c. Kiddie Korral
d. Kids' Harbor
e. Little Lambs
f. Little Stars
g. Lord's Lambs
h. Muppets
i. Noah's Park
j. Pastor's Pals
k. Prairie Pups
l. Rainbow Kids
m. Sonbeams
n. Wee Care

212. Names for Junior Highs
a. A-O.K. Club
b. Bible Lab
c. Christian Soldiers
d. High Voltage
e. Outta Bounds
f. Rock Solid
g. The Lord's Army

213. Names for Senior Highs
a. Chosen Generation
b. Epic Generation
c. High Point
d. Ironworks (Proverbs 27:17)
e. The Crossing
f. The Edge
g. The Quest

214. Have a sign, **"Children are not the church of the future, they are the church of the present."**

215. Have a sign **"Children who are brought into Sunday school are seldom brought up in court."**

216. Have a sign **"You never know if you have another Billy Graham in your class."**

217. Have volunteers to relieve teachers for four Sundays during the summer.

218. Have teachers in training to serve on a rotating basis two weeks on, four weeks off.

219. Have kids draw pictures of the church and post in the narthex.

220. Have students complete memory verses and each receive a certificate of completion.

221. Have the perfect attenders (for year or quarter) listed in the bulletin.

Vacation Bible School

222. Have puppet training for teachers (and students).

223. Two or three months prior have video of last year's Vacation Bible School—Kids singing, laughing having fun, different activities.

224. Have testimonies by kids, especially funny happenings.

225. Two months before VBS with kids singing in background have cards handed out with various opportunities to be checked by volunteers—also cards for needed collectibles.

High School and College Age Ministries

226. Have a band called the "Uth Band".

227. Have a group called **GRAVITY** (**G**od **R**ules **A**nd **V**ictory **I**s **T**otally **Y**ours).

228. Have a program **SNAC** (**S**unday **N**ight **A**fter **C**hurch)

229. When students go off to college, have a business-sized card with the picture and name of the student, college attending, and caption **"Out of Sight, In Our Prayers"** on one side of the card and the student's address away from home, year, new phone number, and favorite "Mail"able Treat on the other side.

CHAPTER 7

Lay Ministries

It is important to train lay members to perform needed tasks, but it is more important to train members to be trainers of others.

To me the biggest difference in the church program of today from that of 50 years ago is the emphasis on small groups within the church. In this chapter are more than 100 names for various groups.

Some of these small groups are cell groups, each having from 3 to 12 people who meet regularly with a common purpose and desire to grow in their relationship with each other and in Christ.

Lay Ministry

230. Have an Annual Senior Award for contribution to both church and community activities.

231. Instead of asking for volunteers, have the Church Board discuss openings and potential leaders and have a committee meet them in their homes.

232. Instead of the term "volunteers" call them 100% involvers.

233. Ask individual members why they are not participating in church work; then take those excuses up with the proper committee and get responses. Then put those excuses on the screen for an evening service and proper response.

234. List openings for volunteer jobs in the bulletin.

235. Have a car ministry where members and others can donate cars in need of repair. Volunteer mechanics with the help of students fix them to be given to the needy, such as someone who lost a job, single mothers, etc.

236. List in the bulletin those members who visited the sick, sent cards, phoned; those who helped someone move; those who baby sat, etc.

237. Have an umbrella ministry where members form an umbrella cover or canopy when it is raining. This is especially helpful for those who are dropped off in front of the church.

238. On a work day, give a raffle ticket for every hour worked.

239. Have a "Lay Person of the Month" selected from nominations.

240. Have a Friendship Visitation Ministry for those who are temporarily or permanently unable to participate in the regular services and activities of the church.

241. In the bulletin list the Shepherd of the Week, name and phone number. The Shepherd of the Week is available to those who have made decisions to accept Christ as Lord and Savior or to attend new membership class.

242. Have an Adopt a Teacher (public school) ministry by offering support and providing assistance in the teacher's classroom or office. Pray daily for your adoptee's needs—wisdom, strength, classroom discipline, time management, and relationship with God. Treat the adoptee to lunch. Give a lending hand in the classroom, read stories, help with arts and crafts, assist students in reading and math. For more information contact Christian Educators Association, International, P.O. Box 41300, Pasadena, CA 91114-8300; (626) 798-1124; FAX:798-2346; www.ceai.org

243. Have an Adopt a School Ministry. Pray for public schools in the area, school board members and Christian educators in your congregation. Along with other local churches, develop a Christian Released Time Education program. This allows students to be released from school for religious instruction. Supply volunteers for individualized tutoring in reading and math. Sponsor after-school activities such as arts and crafts, performing arts, music, or sports. Create a big brother/big sister program. Offer scholarships to fund special programs in which needy students may wish to participate. Contact CEAI (above).

MEN

244. Names for men's groups:

a. **IMG—I**ron **M**en's **G**roup (three to five men meet weekly in a local restaurant an hour before work)

b. **IMF—I**ron **M**en of **F**aith

c. **MAG—M**en's **A**ccountability **G**roup

d. **MEN—M**ale **E**go **N**urturing

e. **MENS—M**en **E**ncouraging and **N**urturing **S**upport

f. **ORG—O**ld **R**etired **G**uys

g. **MAN ALIVE**

h. **STEPHEN MINISTERS**—To pray and counsel with those in need.

WOMEN

245. Names for women's groups:

a. **CLEAN**—**C**itizens **L**eading **E**ffective **A**ction **N**ow—Letter writing campaign for family values in our society.

b. **EWES**—Every **W**oman's **E**nrichment **S**tudies

c. **LAW**—**L**ife **A**fter **W**ork—for women working outside the home.

d. **MOM**—**M**others **O**n the **M**ove

e. **MOPS**—**M**others **O**f **P**re**S**choolers—rekindling the joys of motherhood without getting lost in the endless child demands.

f. **SAS**—**S**ew **A**nd **S**hare (Women's Missionary Group)

g. **WINNERS**— **W**onderfully made **I**ndependent of the world, **N**urtured by the Holy Spirit, **N**eeding one another, **E**ncouraging others, **R**eaching the lost, **S**tudying the Word.

h. **WOW**—**W**omen **O**f the **W**ord

i. **WOW**—**W**omen **O**f **W**orth

j. **CHICK FLICK NIGHT**—every month women meet at the church and go to a movie.

k. **GRUB-N-GAB**—Ladies monthly meeting.

l. **LADIES NIGHT OUT**--Once a month all women are invited to take a break and meet at a restaurant and enjoy a time of fellowship and good food.

m. **LADIES NIGHT OUT**—Two to four times a year get together for fun and fellowship.

n. **MORNING BREAK**—A weekday Bible Study especially for women.

o. **OUT-TO-LUNCH BUNCH**—Meets 11:30-1:00 P.M

p. **PIECEMAKERS**—for women who like to quilt and those who simply want to be with quilters.

q. **TEA AND THERAPY**—Women's support group.

ADULTS

246. Names for adult groups:

a. **AIA**—**A**dults **i**n **A**ction

b. **ALPHA**—**A**ll, without exception, who want to know more about God and grow more; **L**earning and laughter, **P**asta, eating together; **H**elping one another; **A**sk anything—all questions are honored.

c. **FEAST**—**F**ellowship, **E**ncouragement **A**nd **S**upport **T**eam

d. **OASIS**—**O**lder **A**dults **S**till **I**n **S**ervice

e. **POT**—**P**arents **O**f **T**eenagers

f. **TIES**—**T**eamwork **I**nsuring **E**lder **S**upport

g. **TNT**—**T**ried and **T**rue, Geared for adults between the ages of 45 and 65.

h. **CHOSEN AMBASSADORS**

i. **EMPTY NESTERS**—To be with other parents whose children have left home.

j. **HILLTOPPERS**

k. **KEENAGERS**

l. **LIFE LIGHTERS**—a support group for those experiencing grief or loss through death, divorce, or life situations.

m. **PILLARS CLUB**

o. **PRIME TIME GANG**

p. **PRIME TIMERS**—Session for "seasoned citizens" who seek fellowship with others in the prime of their lives, with lunch on the premises.

q. **RECYCLED TEENAGERS**—for those 55 or older

r. **SAINTS ALIVE**—has monthly potlucks and other social activities.

s. **SEAFARERS**—adult social group for couples and singles 50+, organized around nautical terms, and consists of subgroups called ships.

t. **SECOND WIND**

u. **SOJOURNERS**

v. **THE 39ERS**

w. **THE SILVER SPARKS**—all married and singles over 50 years old.

247. MARINERS ADULT FELLOWSHIP GROUPS

a. **Argonauts**—couples and singles, middle age and retirees who are energetic and seek the company of new friends.
b. **Beachcombers**—workers and retirees having grown children who enjoy fellowship, dining, and service projects.
c. **Calypsos**—mostly in the 40-50 age group who enjoy family oriented activities with their children.
d. **Catamarans**—couples seeking to strengthen relationships.
e. **Cee Bees**—retired couples and singles who plan programs for those with free time during the week.
f. **Dolphins**—middle age and retirees who enjoy monthly outings and a yearly weekend at a retreat.
g. **Jellyfish**—newest Mariners seeking adults of any age or marital status who enjoy fun and Christian fellowship.
h. **Minnows**—young adults with babies to elementary age children who have a mixture of family and adult-only events.
i. **Nautilus**—parents and grandparents who are enjoying being "empty nesters."
j. **Outriggers**—mature adults together for a long time who enjoy companionship with those with like interests.

k. **Sandpipers**—seniors who are young at heart who enjoy adventure, new experiences, fun and fellowship.
l. **Spinnakers**—middle age individuals who appreciate the good life now that the kids are out on their own.
m. **Tradewinds**—members who are active in the church—many having teenagers or older children.

YOUNG ADULTS

248. Names for young adult groups:

a. **BRIDGE**—**B**eginning **R**ecovery **I**n **D**ivine and **G**rief **E**xperience

b. **CALL**—**C**hristian **A**ction **L**ife **L**ine (ministry to feed the hungry)

c. **CARE**—**C**ontact **A**nd **R**elate **E**veryone

d. **CIK**—**C**hristians **I**n the **K**now

e. **CLAW**—**C**hristian **L**ife **A**nd **W**itness

f. **CYA**—**C**hristian **Y**oung **A**dults

g. **DAWN**—**D**iscipling **A** **W**hole **N**ation

h. **EDGE**—**E**xtreme **D**iscipleship **G**eneration **E**ncounters

i. **FIT**—**F**amilies **I**n **T**ouch

j. **FOCUS**—**F**riendship for **O**verseas **C**ollege and **U**niversity **S**tudents

k. **HOPE**—**H**ear **O**ur **P**rayers **E**verywhere

l. **ISI**—**I**nternational **S**tudents **I**ncorporated

m. **KYP**—**K**eeping **Y**ou **P**osted

n. **LIFE**—**L**earning Through **I**nstruction, **F**riendship, and **E**vangelism

o. **LIFE**—**L**ove, **I**nstruction, **F**ellowship, **E**ncouragement

p. **LOVE, INC**—**I**n the **N**ame of **C**hrist

q. **PAR**—**P**rayer **A**nd **R**evival

r. **PIC**—**P**artners **I**n **C**hrist

s. **PPT**—**P**rayer, **P**raise, **T**estimony

t. **ROCK**—**R**evelation **O**f **C**hrist's **K**ingdom

u. **SALT**—**S**ervants' **A**dvanced **L**eadership **T**raining

v. **SEND**—**S**tart, **E**vangelize, **N**urture, **D**evelop

w. **SNAP**—**S**aturday **N**ight **A**live **P**rogram

x. **STEP**—**S**ystemic **T**raining for **E**ffectual **P**arenting

y. **TNT**—**T**wenties **A**nd **T**hirties

z. **WINGS**—**W**hen **I**n **N**eed **G**od **S**ustains

OLDER ADULTS

249. Names for older adult groups

a. **Alpha Careers**

b. **Ambassadors**

c. **Baby Boomers**

d. **Carpenters**

e. **Crossroads**

f. **Family Focus** (for those having difficulty raising children in a society bent on destroying family values)

g. **Firm Foundation**

h. **Friday Night Live**

i. **Harvesters**

j. **Highlifers**

k. **Home Builders**

l. **Home Improvement**

m. **Joint Heirs**

n. **Life Partners**

o. **Life Seekers**

p. **Next Generation**

q. **Pace Setters**

r. **Positive Parenting**

s. **Redeemer Care Group**

t. **Redeemer Care Group** (for the addicted and their loved ones.)

u. **Revised Edition**

v. **Seekers**

w. **The Grape Vine** (Joys and concerns which the congregation should know about and pray about)

x. **Zephyrs**

SINGLE ADULTS

250. Singles

a. **CASTLE—C**hristian **A**ssociation of **S**ingles **T**ogether for **L**ove and **E**ncouragement.

b. **SALSA—S**ingles **A**s **L**iving **S**ingles **A**gain.

c. **SAM—S**ingle **A**dult **M**inistries

d. **SLICK—S**ingles **L**iving **I**n **C**hrist's **K**ingdom.

e. **SNAP—S**aturday **N**ight **A**live **P**rogram.

f. **SPN—S**ingle **P**arenting **N**etwork.

g. **20/20**—Singles who desire to know, understand, and practice the Word of God

h. **Beachcombers**—for singles born from 1950-1960

i. **Compass Points**

j. **Flying Solos**

k. **Free Spirits**

l. **Heir Time**

m. **His Generation**

n. **Impact**—single career-aged people pursuing vocational goals

o. **Islanders**—for singles born after 1955.

p. **Shipmates**—for singles born from 1935-1955

q. **Single Focus**—for unmarried persons in their 40's and 50's who are looking for warm authentic fellowship, strong Biblical teaching and one-on-one caring in a group of young-at-heart friends.

r. **Singles Alive**

s. **Singleship**—for singles born before 1945

t. **Singletarians** (for older singles)

u. **Wave Runners**—for singles born after 1965.

CHAPTER 8

Church Bulletins

IIf all the ideas in this chapter were to be used, no bulletin would be big enough to contain them. But you might find two or three you can use.

Rather than having the announcements in the bulletin, many churches have them on the screen before the service, during the service, or after the service. This can save much valuable time.

If volunteers put out the church bulletin, they should be recognized from time to time. Few people realize how much time and effort are needed to produce a church bulletin. The selection of the bulletin, or worship folder, should be made with care. One church I visited had an elaborate and expensive-looking bulletin cover with the name of the donor listed.

Church Bulletin

251. Instead of *Church Bulletin* call it
  a. *Worship Folder*
  b. *Program Folder*
  c. *Worship Celebration*

252. Have the church motto printed in the bulletin.

253. Print a welcome such as, "WELCOME—Peace, Hope, Joy, and Love to All Who Enter Here."

254. In the order of worship have asterisk for "seating of those who have been detained."

255. Have large-print bulletins available for those who find them useful.

256. At bottom of first page: "Please turn off cell phones, pagers, and other communication devices."

257. Instead of "Announcements" call it "Opportunities"

258. Instead of "Announcements" call it "Special Happenings"

259. Put the Pastor's day off in the bulletin.

Messages to Visitors

260. Our Pastor would love to meet you. He will be available at the front of the stage following the services.

261. We'd like to help you. If you would like to know how to become a Christian, simply make a note on the Silent Roll Card enclosed in your Program Folder. Pastor personally reads every card, and he will mail materials to help you grow spiritually. Sharing your decision with someone is an important first step.

262. Your presence here today is your gift to us. Please do not feel you must make further contributions.

263. To enhance your worship experience, we offer several features to make your time at (name of church) a memorable one.

264. We warmly welcome all who have come to worship with us today. Each day we live is a precious gift of God, loaded with possibilities to learn something new and gain fresh insights into His great truths. Please fill out the visitors' card, and if we can help you in any way, let us know.

265. Good Morning! God's Words instruct us to enter His gates with praise. It is always good to come to God's house. We welcome you to our house of worship today. It is our prayer that you will be met with God's love and you will be encouraged. Please complete a visitor's card and place it in the offering plate. That will be your gift to us.

266. Thanks for checking us out! Hey, we're glad you came. We want to serve you better, so please take a moment to fill out the communication card and place it in the container. Kick back, relax, and enjoy the service. We feel privileged that you chose to worship with us today. Please stop by the Welcome Table for more information about our church.

267. We are blessed to have you worship with us today. Please give us the opportunity to get to know you by joining us in the Coffee Hour following the service.

268. Visitors, you are invited to a reception in your honor following the service in (location). We'd love to meet you.

269. **W**orship the Lord in the beauty of holiness. I Chron 16:29
Enter His gates with thanksgiving. Ps. 100:4
Look to Jesus, the author and finisher of our faith. Heb 12:2
Come before His presence with singing. Ps. 100:2
Observe and remember the Sabbath to keep it holy. Ez.20:8
Make a joyful noise unto the Lord. Ps. 66:1
Enjoy praising God with God's people. Ps 67:3

Messages to Parents

270. We encourage the presence of your wonderful, wiggly children in our worship service.

271. To get the most out of your visit may we recommend: Trust your children to the care of our dedicated, loving workers! We have care for all during our Worship Service. Greeters in the narthex will direct you to the nursery. We also have children's church during the latter part of the service for 4 years through 2nd grade.

272. PARENTS WITH CHILDREN DURING WORSHIP SERVICES: Infants and Toddlers up to age 4 can be placed in our fully serviced nursery; or, if necessary, parents can sit with their children in the Assembly Room off the worship center where the worship service can be viewed on closed circuit TV.

273. Children's coloring bulletins, crayons, and Bible story books are available at the back of the sanctuary for the use of your children during worship services.

274. Parents, you are encouraged to take your children to their classes or nursery facilities while you are in the Celebration Services. If your child must stay with you due to illness, we have provided a closed circuit TV room where you can watch the service in its entirety.

275. Infants and toddlers are welcome in the worship service. However, if parents would like, their young children may be taken care of during worship by a competent adult. Such care is provided free of charge. Just let an usher know if you would like this service.

Messages to Worshippers

276. Our church strives to be inclusive in its worship and community life. You are encouraged to use whichever gender you find most meaningful in the nouns and pronouns of the hymns and liturgy.

277. At the asterisks please rise in body and spirit as you are able.

278. The congregation is invited to stand as instructed, but please feel free to remain seated.

279. Altar flowers are given to the glory of God by (name of donor).

280. Flowers today are given by (Name of donor) in celebration of (person's) birthday on (date).

281. To donate flowers, please call (name), (phone number), our flower lady.

282. The Lord's Prayer...we say "debts."

Bulletin Inserts

283. Have different colored inserts for faster reference.

284. Call the newsletter
- a. From Parson to Person
- b. From the Pastor's Pen
- c. News From the Pews
- d. Church Family News

285. List names of members committed to reading the Bible through the year. Use a form to identify readers. "I have completed the reading for (Month). Please include my name on the HONOR ROLL for this month."—signed, (name).

286. Look At Our Faithfulness
Worship attendance previous Sunday_________
Giving previous Sunday____________
Weekly giving to meet budget___________
Annual operating budget_______________

287. Soul Winning Stats
Soulwinners_________
Doors knocked_______
Souls saved__________

288. Outline of sermon

289. Memory verse for week/month

290. Each week's schedule for "Through the Bible In One Year."

291. Scripture reading in insert so everyone can follow along, and with the same version.

292. Acknowledge by name those who have served in a special way.

293. Names of those participating in today's service.

294. All-church prayer calendar for the month, each day listing a specific need.

CHAPTER 9

Visitors

How visitors are treated often determines whether or not they return. At one or two churches I visited the members seemed and acted as though they had been baptized in vinegar as they related to the visitor, or even to one another.

At one church I arrived between the Sunday School and the worship service. I sat for ten minutes while people walked by me as if I did not exist. Then a lady came and sat next to me; and I found out that she, too, was a visitor.

Public recognition of visitors from the pastor or worship leader varies from church to church. I attended one all black church where the pastor had all visitors stand and give their names. He made it clear that there wasn't time for speeches; and when it came for me to introduce myself, I stated my name and then said, "I guess you all will never know what this white dude is doing here in this all black church." With that, the pastor allowed me to state my mission and to compliment the black churches for respecting God's house enough to dress properly.

Some churches do not recognize visitors personally and publicly, feeling that they would feel more comfortable if they are allowed to remain anonymous.

VISITORS

295. Have another name for visitors
  a. Guests
  b. First Time Worshippers
  c. Newcomers

296. In the parking lot have two places next to handicapped spaces for "First-time Visitors."

297. Poll the members to find out which members of the church would make good greeters.

298. Have an appointed church growth task force to find out ways to attract visitors.

299. Have a "Doorkeeper" ministry involved in the care and support of those who come the first time. This area includes Greeters, Ushers, Information Desk, Visitors' Reception and Tracking Team.

300. Have a training session for greeters.

301. Trained greeters serve at least one month so they can recognize visitors who come again.

302. Greeters remember names and faces of visitors as they come to the service, and after the service call them by name and express appreciation for their coming to worship.

303. Greeters try to tell if a visitor might want public recognition in the worship service, and relays this indication to the pastor.

304. Teach the young people to be friendly with visitors.

305. Have members take responsibility of meeting visitors near them. First introduce themselves to the visitor and then introduce them to another member of the church.

306. At a church dinner have a role play for the wrong way to greet visitors and then the right way.

307. Have welcome table outside not only for visitors but also for members who want information or have prayer requests.

308. Have a label machine to print names of visitors.

309. Before the service, the pastor greets everyone, especially visitors, in the narthex.

310. Give everyone (members, regular attenders, guests) a name tag so newcomers will feel comfortable. Different color for visitors.

311. Have the official church welcome to visitors in the bulletin.

Bulletin Notices

312. Have a special bulletin for visitors—order of worship, church mission, information about church, programs, activities, etc.

313. You are welcome in this place. Pastor (Name) thanks you for coming to our church. We are a full gospel, Spirit-filled family fellowship where people of all denominations are welcome to worship God in Spirit and in Truth. The music is lively, the worship is sincere, and the message is positive. God's Word, the Bible, is the source of all our teaching and preaching. Jesus Christ, God's Son, is our Savior and Head of this church.

314. WE WELCOME you in Jesus' name. May your joy be full as we come together. A WARM WELCOME TO OUR VISITORS. We are glad you have joined us. We ask that everyone sign a worship card and place it in the offering plate. All baptized persons who desire to receive Christ through Holy Communion are invited to participate in the Sacrament.

315. You are welcome, just as you are. All are welcome at (Name) Church. You truly matter to us because you matter to God. We understand ourselves as Christians in worship, study, and service; and affirming each person's unique gifts and talents, we invite you into a loving and prayerful relationship with God. If you want to know more about our church or about Christianity, please indicate so on the Registration Pad as it is passed in your pew. If there is information that you feel would help us better serve you, please indicate this. We honor and celebrate your decision to be here!

316. A number of new faces are evident in our worshipping community each Sunday. We are indeed pleased to welcome you particularly, and invite you **IF YOU ARE SEEKING A NEW CHURCH**

HOME, to consider membership in the life and witness and ministry of this exciting downtown Church. We invite you to share your insight and gifts of time, talent, and substance in our midst so that the possibilities of our total ministry can be enhanced and expanded. We receive you as gifts of God in our midst to be acknowledged and utilized in the ministry of this place.

317. WELCOME! The (Name) Church is here to be a friendly assembly where you enter the truth of God's word, where Jesus is Lord, where your spiritual needs are met, and where friendships are established.

318. We are thankful that you have joined us today. We trust God will minister to you during our service and that you will sense God's love through His people today. If you are a visitor to our fellowship, please do not feel obligated to participate in the offering.

319. WORSHIP NOTES—Welcome to worship at (Name) Church! If you are a visitor with us this morning, please sign a *Voice From The Pew* card available in the pew and introduce yourself to the pastor. If there is any way we can be of service to you, please let us know. God bless you in your worship today.

320. Welcome to our service of worship and praise. *"This is the day the Lord hath made."* Visitors, please register your worship and communion attendance (cards in pew rack) and kindly sign our guest book.

321. Visitors, welcome to our worship service. May the Spirit of God strengthen and deepen your faith in Jesus Christ as you hear God's Word today. Please leave us a record of your visit by filling out a *Welcome Worshiper* card, and feel free to call on the pastor at any time.

322. Welcome: We appreciate your coming to worship with us today. Please join with us as we seek the presence of our Lord Jesus Christ in Worship, learn more of Him in Bible study and prayer, experience His love in fellowship, and carry on His work in evangelism and service to others. We want you to experience God's love this morning, a love that is real and free. We pray that we can help you towards that end this morning. If you don't know Jesus as your Savior and Lord, we would like to introduce you to Him and help you grow as His disciple. Please talk to any of the staff about your needs in this area.

323. WELCOME to Our Church. We are happy to have you worship with us today, and we hope that we shall see you again. Please fill in the reverse side of this card and place it in the offering plate or hand it to one of the ushers in order that we may serve you further.

324. We're glad you are here and hope you have a great experience in this morning's Celebration Service. So we can better know how to serve you, please take a moment to fill out the Communication Card and place it in the offering basket at the end of the service.

325. Welcome! Your presence in worship here is an honor and joy. We pray that your heart is open, the Word is clear, and that you go out from this place refreshed. You are encouraged to participate in the Prelude as a time for silent prayer and meditation. After Worship you are invited to meet in a circle in front of the communion table for discussion with your fellow worshippers and our pastor.

326. Please sign the visitors registration card. We promise we will not abuse the information—we won't sell your name to any listing company.

327. Please sign the visitors' card. We won't use your signature to forge checks; and we won't call you every day to see if you are coming back.

328. Welcome, Friends and Guests! You are our friends in Christ. We are happy you are worshipping the Lord God with us this morning. Please sign our Guest Book and come back again. May the joy of our Lord Jesus Christ be yours today and always.

329. Welcome, Visitors! We hope you find worship to be meaningful for you, and you will join us again. If you are seeking a church home/family, we hope you will consider (Name) Church. Please speak with the pastor if you are interested in membership.

330. Welcome to (Name) Church. We hope your experience of worship and friendship with us will provide you with hope and renewal. Please join the other worshipper, noting your attendance with us in the blue friendship folders. We invite you to join us following worship for **fellowship and refreshment** in (location).

331. RELAX!--No matter what your previous church experience may be, it's our hope that today's service will be a fresh and positive encounter with God's love and power for your life. Thanks for coming.

332. We Welcome you In the Name of JESUS The peace of the Lord Jesus be with you. You are among friends. We pray that this will be a time of rest and refreshment for you, and that you will receive strength and encouragement as you worship the Lord with us today. *Our special welcome to you who are here for the first time.* We invite you to sign our guest book on the Welcome Table in the Narthex, and to join us for coffee and fellowship after the service. Thank you for being here. Everyone here, at one time, was a visitor. They came back. We hope you will too.

333. Relax..Enjoy. We trust that you will be uplifted by the love, acceptance, and truth of God which is shared here today. It is our desire to worship our living God authentically, and to let Him minister to us and through us as He sees fit this morning. Guests always make our worship service more enjoyable.

334. Welcome to (Name of) Church. Today, it is our desire to worship our loving God Who gave us Jesus Christ, our Savior. We are glad that you are with us. It is our prayer that God will minister to you in just the way you need to be blessed today. We trust that you will experience the love and grace of the spiritual family of our church and that you will also be an extension of that love and grace. May the Lord make His face to shine on you.

335. WELCOME VISITORS. Thank you for worshipping with us. Here are four ways to get to know us better. **(l) Visitor's packet:** These packets describe our faith, practice and ministries and are available from an usher or at the Information Booth. **(2) Information Booth:** This booth, located on the patio, is staffed with friendly people to answer your questions. **(3) Visitors' Open House:** The third Sunday of each month after each service in the Fireside Room upstairs. **(4) Pastor's Class:** Our pastor will lead this class for those who would like to learn more about our church.

336. We offer a **SPECIAL WELCOME** to each of our **FIRST-TIME AND REPEAT VISITORS** worshipping with us today. If you are looking for a church home where the Holy Ghost is no stranger and where Jesus is the Head of The House, you are at the right place. Welcome Home!

337. Visitors, please do not hurry out after the service. Give our people a chance to greet you. If you are looking for a church home, your search is over. *"Come, thou, with us and we will do thee good."*

338. Worship—Ps 95:6
Enter—Ps. 100:4
Lord—Ps. 92:13
Come into His Presence with joy—Ps. 100:2
Obey—I John 5:2
Merciful—Ps. 103:8
Eternal—John 3:15

Greeters

339. Instead of "Greeters" call them "Hosts" or "Hostesses."

340. Have two sets of greeters—one at the church entrance, and one at another section of the sanctuary or in the parking lot.

341. Have greeters for (l) young people, (2) middle-aged, (3) seniors.

342. Have those members sitting next to visitors be the greeters to introduce them to the congregation.

343. Greeters take names of visitors as they go in and give the names to the pastor so he can introduce them to the congregation.

Visitors' Participation

344. Sign the "Who's Who" Book.

345. Fill out a "Guest Survey" card with regular information needed, plus *"Would you return? ___Yes; ___No; ___Maybe."* Encourage guests to fill it out after the service or to mail it in.

346. Have a rating postcard with stamp and address of church, example, with 5 as the highest rating:

Welcome and Friendliness:	**5**☐	**4**☐	**3**☐	**2**☐	**1**☐
Facilities:.............................	**5**☐	**4**☐	**3**☐	**2**☐	**1**☐
Music:.................................	**5**☐	**4**☐	**3**☐	**2**☐	**1**☐
Preaching...........................	**5**☐	**4**☐	**3**☐	**2**☐	**1**☐

Introducing Visitors

347. Greeters get names of visitors before they enter sanctuary then give to pastor, who later introduces them to the worshippers.

348. In a smaller church, do not embarrass visitors. They may be a pulpit committee scouting for a possible candidate as their pastor.

349. If visitors are brought by church members, the members introduce them to the congregation during the service and to other members after the service.

350. Pastor, "If you feel comfortable, please stand and introduce yourselves."

351. Ask all visitors to stand and remain standing until the pastor goes down and personally greets them and tells the congregation their names and where they are from.

352. When the pastor or visitors say their names, everyone says "Hi, (First Name)."

353. After the introduction, pastor says, "And we all say **'WELCOME'**."

354. After the introduction, pastor says, "Let's all say **'HONORED GUESTS'**."

355. When publicly inviting visitors to return ALSO invite members and regular attenders to return..

356. After recognizing the visitors, have congregation sing a "Welcome" song composed by one of the members.

357. Have people from another church evaluate the way visitors are treated.

Gifts

358. First-time visitors, raise your hands, so our ushers may give you a gift, or you may pick it up in the foyer.

359. If you did not take a rose when you came into the sanctuary, please take one when you leave.

360. Have a packet with information about the church—map of facilities, statement of faith, group ministries, nursery, a tract on salvation, the importance of Sunday School, pastor's business card/church card, and have a life savor taped to packet.

361. This coupon entitles you to a FREE cup of coffee or one of the following items for being our guest today:
□*Expresso* □*Cappuccino* □*Latte* □*Mocha* □*Hot Chocolate* □*Hot Tea*

362. More samples of gifts:

a. Bible, compliments of the church and donated by (name of donor).
b. Hand-made wooden cross on stand with the church name and address.
c. Gold cross lapel pin.
d. Gold cross embroidered applique to be pressed on the garment.
e. Red heart to be worn on lapel or dress so members can see and welcome guests.
f. Pen with the church name.
g. Mug with the church name.
h. Ten-minute video of the church using member involvement.
i. Bookmark with information about the church and a Scripture, such as Ps. 84:4
j. Picture postcard showing picture of church and short history.
k. Magnetic card with church name, address, phone number, worship service times, "**Visitors always welcome**."
l. Sack of cookies in the foyer.

Follow-up

363. Pastor welcomes visitors at the END of the service. (This does not encroach on the service).

364. If visitors respond to introduction during worship service, remember something about what they said in greeting them after service.

365. Have the names of last Sunday's visitors in the bulletin.

366. Have members invite visitors home for lunch.

CHAPTER 10

Greeting One Another

Almost all churches now have a few minutes during the worship service for the worshippers to greet one another. This practice was not so common 50 years ago. In this chapter you will find different ways of greeting each other and different times of greeting.

A greeter is a special type of minister. Greeters should be carefully selected and trained

.

GREETING ONE ANOTHER

What

367. Instead of "Greeting One Another", Call it

a. Greetings and Salutations
b. Passing of the Peace
c. Ritual of Friendship
d. The Sharing of the Peace
e. Time of Greeting

When

368. Greet one another during prelude.

369. Greetings just before children's sermon.

370. Greetings while children are dismissed for their own church service.

371. Have the Greeting immediately following the recognition of guests.

How

372. Worship team goes down to greet everyone.

373. In smaller congregation have pastor come down and greet visitors.

374. Sing a happy song or chorus during greetings.

375. Give neighbor a " Hello, a Handshake, or a Hug." Or

376. a "Handshake, a High Five, or a Hug"

377. Have certain members seek out visitors.

378. Have choir sing a lively song during greetings.

379. Once or twice a year ask neighbor's middle name.

380. Greet one another as if a long lost brother or sister.

381. Give a High Five, then say "You can make a difference."

382. Say "You're not getting older, you're getting better."

383. Tap someone on the shoulder and say, "I'm so glad you're here."

384. Tell each other how lucky they are to be here.

385. As you greet one another, say "Peace be with you"

386. Each Sunday have a different handshake

a. Regular hand shake
b. Pump hand shake
c. Model T Ford shake
d. Japanese style (shake own hands, bow down three times
e. Fisherman's style (limp hand shake, wiggle back and forth)
f. Paul Bunyan hand shake (each grabbing his/her own right thumb with the left hand as if working a two-man saw)
g. Have members think of different handshakes

CHAPTER 11

Worship Service

In this chapter are some messages to worshippers which may appear in the bulletin or on the screen or be announced from the podium. The same can be said for the announcements.

Originally, each call to worship was an idea in itself, but to reduce the number of ideas in this book to 1001 the 40 calls to worship are listed as two, with 38 sub ideas.

A few churches did not have their order of worship in the bulletin. This may have been acceptable to the regular attenders, but it is confusing to the visitor.

WORSHIP SERVICE

Messages to Worshippers

387. As we gather for worship, please take a few moments for quiet personal reflection and preparation. Your silence before worship and your warm hospitality afterward are a gracious gift to others. May God bless you in His service.

388. Enter to pray....Stay to worship....Go to serve.

389. Approach this service as if it were the last Sunday before the Coming of Christ. We enter the sanctuary in an attitude of meditation and prayer. Let us prepare for another visitation from God's Spirit. (Please turn off all cell phones and pagers)

390. As you enter the sanctuary, we invite you to enjoy greeting one another. Then, during the prelude, in consideration of those who wish to prepare for worship in silence, we request that you make prayer and meditation your primary concern.

391. Have the right worship attitude:
Before the service, talk to God
During the service, let God talk to you
After the service, talk to each other.

392. Please sit down and enjoy preparing for worship with the music that is being played. Take a moment to focus on the Lord. May your hearts and minds be full of His peace this morning.

393. As a matter of reverence and courtesy, please note that noise and movement during the service are a distraction to others around you. If you must leave the service early, please sit in the back rows. Parents with young children are requested to use the nursery. If it is preferable for your child to stay with you, please sit in the back so you can slip out easily should your child find it difficult to sit quietly.

394. Stuffed animals and coloring books are available at the back of the church for children to use in the back pews during the service. The materials are there for the purpose of helping children with worship, and are to be returned to the basket after the service.

395. To enhance your worship experience, we have provided special features for you: A wireless Hearing Assistance System (available at the Sound Booth), A sound-proof Cry Room to which you can take a fussy child, and yet hear and observe the entire worship service, A beautiful nursery staffed with loving, trained care-providers for your little one.

396. As you enter to worship, you are invited to come forward and light a candle for yourself and/or someone you know in need of prayer.

397. Please note: Our services last about 90 minutes. We desire to provide a distraction-free worship service. For this reason, please observe the following guidelines: Families with small children not in the nursery or children's ministry are encouraged to sit in the back rows of the auditorium. Once the message has begun, entry (or re-entry) into the auditorium will be limited to back row seating. Thank you for helping us facilitate a fruitful time of worship!

398. Service Etiquette—We are here today to honor God and to seek to know Him. In order to facilitate an atmosphere of worship, we would encourage you to limit your moving about during the service. **We ask that you remain seated during the service. If you do need to leave the auditorium, please do so between program sequences.** To minimize distraction please turn off cell phones and pagers (or activate 'vibration' mode) while in the service. **We also remind you that quality nursery, toddler, and school-age children's programs are provided in the Children's Wing.** If you prefer to bring your child to the service, please sit toward the rear of the auditorium. If your child cries or is distracting, a TV monitor is available in the lobby for your convenience. Thank you!

399. (Name of) Church strives to be inclusive in its worship and community life. You are encouraged to use whichever gender you find most meaningful in the nouns and pronouns of the hymns and liturgy.

400. Allow greeting and conversing until the music begins. Start worshipping with the first note of music. As the organist/pianist plays, let us observe a holy hush that each may prepare to praise God.

401. The Bible declares that Jesus Christ is present whenever two or more Christians gather in His name (Mt. 18:20). The Bible also declares that God is King of Kings (I Tim. 6:15). We therefore stand in the presence of Christ our King as a way of honoring and acknowledging His presence. However, if your physical condition makes standing uncomfortable, please feel free to remain seated.

402. Children older than Third Grade are invited to attend worship with their parents. Have welcome message on screen before service.

Policy

403. Have the ushers stand half way down to front with bulletins to get people to sit toward the front.

404. For small crowd have back half of auditorium roped off, or one side. The pastor comes down from the platform.

405. If overcrowded, ask people to move to middle of the pews so ushers can seat late comers.

406. Have no seating during prayer, special music, or sermon.

407. The first Sunday of the month is Birthday Sunday. All having birthdays that month go forward and all sing, "Happy Birthday."

408. Have name tags or buttons on board with their names behind. This will be not only an indication of church membership and identification, but also will show those members who are not present.

409. Have coffee BEFORE the service for (1) easier to find a parking space, (2) keep awake during service, (3) socialize before the service allowing early exit after the service.

410. Have coffee AFTER the service so worshippers will be fully awake driving home.

411. Have a wheelchair available for the handicapped.

412. Have a large Bible brought in and placed on the pulpit or in front, affirming the service is Scripturally founded; and at the end of the service the Bible is taken from the front and placed on a stand at the main exit symbolizing the Word going with the worshippers.

413. In honoring newborns and their parents have blue flowers for boys and pink flowers for girls—and anniversary cups for those having anniversaries.

Preparing For Worship

414. Instead of "Worship Service" call it "Celebration Service"

415. Instead of "Worship Service", call it "Elements of Celebration"

416. Have the early morning service called "Service of Prayer and Power."—No sermon, no offering plate passed, but plate in back for those who want to give.

417. In order not to be exclusive, call it "Early Service" rather than "Contemporary Service."

418. Name the one in charge of the service

a. Worship leader
b. Officiant
c. Celebrant
d. Director

419. Instead of testing the mike as 1, 2, 3, recite a Scripture.

420. During football season, **"ARE YOU READY FOR SOME WORSHIP?"**

Calls to Worship

421. Scriptural Calls to Worship

a. *"I will extol the Lord at all times, His praise will always be on my lips."* Ps. 34:1

b. *"Enter His gates with thanksgiving and His courts with praise; give thanks to Him and praise His name."* Ps. 100:4

c. *"...Shout unto God with a voice of triumph."* Ps. 47::1 (Also Ps. 50:23; 104:1, 119:164, 139:14)

d. *"Surely God is in this place. This is none other than the house of God."* Gen. 28:16,17

e. *"Give thanks and call upon God's name. Make known God's deeds among the peoples. Sing praises. Tell of God's wonderful works."* I Chron. 16:8, 9

f. *"Blessed are you, O God, forever and ever. Yours, O God, are the greatness, the power, the glory, the victory and the majesty; for all that is in the heavens and on earth is yours. You are exalted as head above all."* I Chron. 29:10:11

g. *"It is good to give thanks to God, to sing praises to your name, O Most High, to declare your steadfast love in the morning, and your faithfulness by night."* Ps. 92:1-2

h. *"Come, let us sing to God. Let us make a joyful noise to the rock of our salvation! Let us come into God's presence with thanksgiving. Let us make a joyful noise with songs of praise."* Ps. 95:1-2

i. *"Come, let us worship and bow down. Let us kneel before the Lord, our Maker For the Lord is our God, and we are the people of God's pasture, and the flock that is led by God's hand."* Ps. 95:6,7

j. *"O sing to God a new song. Sing to God, all the earth. Sing and bless God's name. Tell of salvation from day to day. Declare God's glory among the nations, and the marvelous works of God among all the peoples. For great is God and greatly to be praised."* Ps. 96:1-4

k. *"Give thanks to God, for God is good. God's steadfast love endures forever, and God's faithfulness to all generations."* Ps.100:4-5

l. *"Give thanks to God. Make known God's deeds among the peoples. Sing, sing praises to God. Tell of all God's wonderful works. Let the hearts of those who seek their Creator rejoice."* Ps. 105:1-3

m. *"Praise God! Blessed be the name of God from this time on and forevermore. From the rising of the sun to its setting, the name of God is to be praised."* Ps. 113:1-3

n. *"This is the day that God has made. Let us rejoice and be glad in it. Blessed is the one who comes in the name of the Lord."* Ps. 118:24,26

o. "Our help is in the name of God, who made heaven and earth." Ps. 124:8

p. *"Praise God! How good it is to sing praises to our God, for God is gracious; and a song of praise is fitting."* Ps. 147:1

q. *"Praise God! Praise God in the sanctuary. Praise God in the mighty firmament! Praise God for mighty deeds. Praise God's surpassing greatness! Let everything that breathes praise God! Praise God!"* Ps 150-2,6

r. *"Give thanks! Call on God's name. Make known God's deeds among the nations. Sing praises to God, for God has done gloriously. Let this be known in all the earth. Shout aloud and sing for joy, for great in your midst is the Holy One."* Is. 12:4-6

s. *"You are worthy, our God, to receive glory and honor and power, for you created all things, and by your will they existed and were created."* Rev. 4:11

t. *"Amen! Blessing and glory and wisdom and thanksgiving and honor and power and might be to our God forever and ever! Amen."* Rev. 7:12

u. Glory to God the Creator and to Christ and to the Holy Spirit as it was in the beginning, is now and shall be forever and ever. Amen.

v. Blessed are you, O God, who has given to humankind the insight and knowledge to understand your wonders, to discern your truth, to tell forth your abundant mercies., Blessed are you, O God.

w. We praise you, O God. We acknowledge you to be the ruler over all. All the earth worships you. God everlasting.

x. Holy, holy, holy, Lord God of hosts; heaven and earth are full of your glory. Glory be to you, O God most high. Amen.

422. Responsive Calls To Worship

a. **Pastor:** Sing to God a new song; sing to God, all the earth.
Congregation: Sing to God, bless God's name. Tell of salvation from day to day.

b. **Pastor:** Magnify the Lord with me, and let us exalt the Lord's name together.
Congregation: Hallelujah! For the Lord our God the Almighty reigns. Let us rejoice and exult and give God the glory. Ps. 34:3; Rev. 19:6-7

c. **Pastor:** Come, let us sing to God. Let us make a joyful noise to the rock of our salvation!
Congregation: Let us come into God's presence with thanksgiving. Let us make a joyful noise with songs of praise. Ps. 95:1-2

d. **Pastor**: When we turn from the world to enter this time of worship, we are not turning our backs upon hurts and sufferings and evil that surround us.
Congregation: We come here like a person who stops to study a map before going on a perilous journey. We are here to find our way in a lost world. We have come to learn how to do our work as Christians between Sundays.

e. **Pastor:** For all the energy and effort that we can muster, we have learned that it is not enough. The sins of the world are greater than our human strength.
Congregation: And so, first and foremost, we are here to worship the God who not only has come into our midst but who has also called us into mission. Help us, O God, to lift our hearts in praise and to live our lives in faith.

f. **Pastor**: The hand of God rests upon this community.
Congregation: We will be a shelter, a present help in the midst of the storm.

g. **Pastor:** Our God is present.
Congregation: God's healing and liberation will flow from us!

h. **Pastor**: We are the good community of the Loving God!
Congregation: In hope, in joy, in struggle and in certainty, we move with the rhythmic breath of the Holy Spirit—to pray—to love—to work. Amen.

i. **Pastor**: Dear friends, our universe and every universe beyond, blaze and dance, leap and laugh, as never before, because of Easter—
Congregation: Christ's victory over death—the new creation!

j. **Pastor**: So let us have a festival and follow him across the starry heavens and down city streets.
Congregation: Let us have him come to us, to live in us, and to start things all over again.

k. **Pastor:** God, you spin the whirling planets;
Congregation: You fill the seas and spread the plain.
Pastor: God, you mold the mountains and fashion blossoms.
Congregation: You call forth sunshine, wind, and rain.
Pastor: God, your word is still creating, calling us to life made new.
Congregation: Now reveal to us fresh vistas where there's work to dare and do.
Pastor: You have called us to be faithful in our life and ministry.
Congregation: Let us respond in grateful worship, joined in one community!

l. **Pastor:** I will bless the Lord at all times, his praise shall continually be in my mouth.
Congregation: My soul shall make her boast in the Lord; the humble shall hear thereof, and be glad.

m. **Pastor**: O magnify the Lord with me, and let us exalt his name together
Congregation: I sought the Lord and he heard me, and delivered me from all my fears.

n. **Pastor:** Christ came to bring us salvation and has promised to come again. Let us pray that we may always be ready to welcome him.
Congregation: May Jesus' hope come into our lives.
Pastor: That the keeping of Advent may open our hearts to God's love.
Congregation: May Jesus' hope come into our lives.
Pastor: That the light of Christ may penetrate the darkness of sin.
Congregation: May Jesus' hope come into our lives.
Pastor: That the Christmas season may fill us with peace and joy as we strive to follow the example of Jesus.
All: Loving God, your Church joyfully awaits the coming of its Savior, who enlightens our hearts and dispels the darkness of ignorance and sin. Pour forth your blessings upon us as we light the candles of this wreath. May their light reflect the splendor of Christ, for ever and ever. Amen.

Orders of Worship

423.

WORSHIP IN PRAISE
WORSHIP IN MISSIONARY REPORTS
WORSHIP IN SCRIPTURE READING
WORSHIP IN PRAYER
WORSHIP IN HYMNS
WORSHIP IN SPECIAL MUSIC
WORSHIP IN MESSAGE
WORSHIP IN CLOSING HYMN
WORSHIP IN GIVING
WORSHIP IN CLOSING PRAYER

424. We Prepare for Worship (Prelude, Welcome, Opening Prayer)
We Celebrate in Praise (Congregational singing, Special music)
We Hear the Good News (Children's Sermon, Pastor's Message)
We Respond to the Good News (Song of Response, Offering)
We Take the Good News into the World (Blessing, Postlude)

425. The Gathering (Call to Worship, Welcome, Hymn of Praise, Greeting one Another, Announcements)
The Prayer (Silent Intercession and Thanksgiving, Pastoral Prayer, Lord's Prayer)
The Proclamation (Special music, Scripture Reading, Sermon)
The Giving (Offertory, Doxology, Prayer of Dedication)
The Departure (Hymn of Invitation/Commitment, Benediction, Postlude)

426. We Gather To Praise God (Prelude, Welcome, Announcements, Greetings)
We Listen To God's Word (Scripture Reading, Hymn, Special Music, Sermon)
We Respond To God's Word (Sharing of joys and concerns for prayer, Offering Our Gifts, Doxology)
We Go Forth In God's Name (Hymn, Benediction, Congregational Response: Shalom, Postlude)

427. Gathering In God's Name (Prelude, Greeting and Sharing of Concerns, Call To Worship, Opening Hymn)
Proclaiming God's Word (Children's Time, Hymn, Prayer, Scripture Reading, Sermon, Moment for Silent Reflection)
Giving Thanks To God (Affirmation of Faith, Offering, Doxology, Prayer of dedication and service)
Going Forth In God's Name (Hymn, Charge, with people joining hands, Benediction, Postlude)

428. Service of Praise (Prelude, Introit, Call to Worship, Hymn of Praise, Welcome)
Service of Prayer (Prayer Requests, Call to Prayer, Silent Meditation, Pastoral Prayer, The Lord's Prayer, Prayer Response)
Service of the Word (Hymn of Faith, Giving of Our Gifts, Doxology, Prayer of Dedication, Scripture Reading, Anthem, The Message)
Service of Dedication (Invitational Hymn, Closing Prayer, Postlude)

Announcements

429. Have announcements on overhead screen at the beginning of the service and/or at the end.

430. Ask those who have announcements come forward.

431. Have young people make announcements, getting them involved in worship as well as assured attendance.

432. Have members of the band make announcements.

433. Have different members who are involved in church activities line up on one side of sanctuary; and one by one go to podium or at front, introduce self and connection and announcements.

434. Have soft music played during announcements.

435. "Listen closely—We will not repeat announcements."

436. Following the announcements have a "Mirthful Moment" and tell a joke.

CHAPTER 12

Prayer

This chapter covers different aspects to prayer in the worship service, including a section on "The Lord's Prayer."

Someone has said that prayer is when we talk with God, and meditation is when we listen to God. This thought should be installed in the hearts and minds of the worshippers.

Different types of prayer are listed in this chapter.

PRAYER

437. Have a prayer group called PUSH—**P**ray **U**ntil **S**omething **H**appens.

438. PPT—**P**rayer, **P**raise, **T**estimony

439. PAR—**P**rayer **A**nd **R**evival (Keeping our lives up to par)

440. Adult prayer group called "Firestarters"

441. Have a prayer box in front of church for requests for prayer—to be prayed over the next 30 days.

442. Have a "Needs Board" for members to list their needs.

443. Have a "Prayer Chain" for those who really believe in prayer and will call people. Those who sign up for the prayer chain will pray when emergencies arise. Prayers will remain in print up to three weeks unless notified.

444. Have a "Prayer Line" to listen to prayer requests 24 hours a day, with the number to call for requests and the messages checked daily.

445. Have a "Grace Vine" for joys and concerns which the members should know about and pray.

Invitations to Pray

446. Before the service have worshippers go forward to kneel in prayer.

447. Have worshippers give testimonies on prayers answered. (Have walkers with mikes go through congregation and have limit on number and time).

448. At different times during the service invite all who desire, to leave their seats and come to the front for prayer.

449. After the service have lay pastors and prayer ministry personnel available to talk to anyone with needs.

450. Have a prayer room after worship service for prayers and questions about becoming a Christian.

Prayer Times

451. Close the church office each day from 12 to 1:00 P.M. for prayer, inviting all to come.

452. Have a prayer time Monday-Friday 6:00-7:00 A.M. called Early Morning Prayer at the church.

453. Have a Friday Night Progressive Prayer Meeting, called "Intercession Highways" where all meet at one church, then split up to go to different churches to pray for each other—from 7:00 P.M. to 2:00 A.M.

454. On Thursday mornings at 9:00 A.M. have prayer service for all who can come.

455. Have a Saturday night (8:00-9:00 P.M.) session of prayer for the Sunday service.

Prayer Request Cards

456. Have prayer request cards available—call them
- a. The Prayers of the Congregation.
- b. Church family Card
- c. Pastor's Prayer Card
- d. Prayers of Concern and Thanks
- e. Prayers and Care
- f. Prayers and Celebration
- g. Prayers and Joys
- h. Concerns of Our Church Family
- i. My Prayer Requests

457. After listing prayer requests check on whether to announce or not.

458. Have worshippers list name of person(s) and have them checked if family member friend, co-worker, neighbor.

459. On the card, check to celebrate a special event (anniversary, birthday, accomplishments).

460. On the card, check whether temporary request (not to be listed in the newsletter) or semi-permanent request (to be listed in the newsletter).

461. On the card, have members check, "I will cooperate with you by daily decreeing at least five minutes in prayer and Bible."

462. Have two prayer lists—(1)those in current crisis or urgent need, and (2) those in longer term need.

Prayer Points

463. For evening prayer have the lights dimmed.

464. On the first Tuesday of every month have the church staff review the names on the prayer lists. Give the church telephone number for anyone wishing to add or remove names. Have current list in bulletin with names on the prayer list and in smaller font in parentheses the names of those requesting prayer.

465. After each petition the one praying will conclude with the words, "Lord in your mercy" to which the congregation responds, "Hear our prayer."

Prayers Before Worship (Invocation)

466. O God of the promise, we come this morning to be in your presence, to worship you as a people of faith. God, we confess that sometimes we live as if faith in you is unnecessary, that we can find our way without you. We confess that we sometimes act as if our faith doesn't need to respond to the wounds of our world. We set aside what we know of you, and whatyou ask of us, and do what we think is best. Forgive us for our sins, renew us in our faith, restore us in your sight. In Jesus' name, Amen.

467. God of light, stay with us we pray, as we worship today and as we share the risk and challenge of living our faith. By your powerful Spirit, turn our fear to courage and our confusion to confidence. As your light shined on Jesus at the transfiguration, shine in our hearts and lives, that we might be transfigured according to your will. Amen.

468. Unison Invocation, "God of spirit and flesh, God of heaven and earth, God of grapes and grain, we stretch our arms in need of you. We feed ourselves with gifts from you. We sense your Spirit shining in the sunlight, sailing on the wind, and singing in the souls of each one gathered here. Recreate us in your image as we meet you today. Thank you for your love poured out in Jesus. Let your presence flow through us so we can spread joy in those we meet. Amen.

469. We hear you knocking, O God, as you stand outside the locked doors of our hearts, waiting and wanting to enter. Help us to throw open those doors that in this time of worship you may come in as a living presence and we may offer to you our praise and thanksgiving. Amen.

470. As we worship you, O God, unstop our ears, that we might hear your word. Sweep the cobwebs from our minds, that we may receive your truth. Strengthen our wills, that we may become your true disciples. And warm our hearts, that we may receive a full measure of your love. Amen.

471. Eternal God, who exists from eternity to eternity, and is not at one time or one place because all times and all places are in you, we stand before you frail and mortal. But blessed are you, O God of the universe, for you have made us in your own image and breathed into us your spirit. From our small space and limited time we dare to lift our spirits beyond all time and space to you, the eternal One, to give praise and thanksgiving. We beseech you that in this hour of worship you will come and renew within us an energizing sense of your eternal presence. Amen.

472. God of love and truth, liberate us from cold hearts and wandering minds when we seek to come near to you, that with firm connections and kindly affections we may worship in love and truth. Amen.

473. We desire your presence with us, O God. Still our restless spirits that with quiet minds and reverent hearts we may hear your voice and worthily worship you. Amen.

Congregational Prayers

474. After prayer requests have congregation stand and pray aloud.

475. List families to be prayed for daily by the entire congregation for one week. By praying week by week the whole church family will be bathed in prayer in _________weeks.

476. Ask for names for prayer and then have different members of the congregation pray for the names requested.

477. The leader repeats all spoken prayer requests so all can hear.

478. During time of prayer ask worshippers if they know someone they would like to pray with and then feel free to go to that person—while choir or congregation is singing a familiar hymn.

479. In informal service have groups of three or four gather to pray.

480. Ask those who will pray for a loved one to raise their hands.

481. Have worshippers stand and intercede for a loved one who does not know Jesus as Lord and Savior.

482. Have names of church families for all members to pray for each day of the coming week.

483. Have members pray for someone several times a day for one week.

484. Have a period during the service called "Great Silence and Naming"—the naming part is where worshippers call out the names of a loved one or acquaintance in need of prayer.

485. Have a "Prayer Ventures" calendar insert in the bulletin for each day of the month and a Prayer Ventures meeting to enlist prayer requests from members.

Pastoral Prayer

486. Before prayer, read quotations about prayer.

487. Have soft music during the morning prayer but no music during the Lord's Prayer.

488. Before prayer, "Please join me in the spirit of prayer."

489. Open the prayer with "Good morning, Lord."

490. During the prayer everyone holds hands.

491. Close the prayer with, "Lord, please hear our prayers as we silently confess our sins to you."

492. After the morning prayer have congregation pray silently or out loud.

Responsive Prayers

493. Pastor: Declare God's glory among the nations and God's marvelous works among all the people.
Congregation: For great is God and greatly to be praised. Ps. 96-1-4

494. Pastor: Enter God's gates with thanksgiving and God's courts with praise. Give thanks; bless God's name.
Congregation: For God is good. God's steadfast love endures forever and God's faithfulness to all generations. Ps. 100:4, 5

495. Pastor: Praise God, all you nations! Extol God, all you people.
Congregation: For great is God's steadfast love toward us, and God's faithfulness endures forever, Praise God! Ps. 117

496. Pastor: You are worthy, our God, to receive glory and honor and power; for you created all things, and by your will they existed and were created.
Congregation: Holy, Holy, Holy, the Lord God, the Almighty who was and is and is to come, you are worthy to receive glory and honor and power.

497. Pastor: Praise our God, all you who are God's servants.
Congregation: Hallelujah! For the Lord our God, the Almighty reigns. Let us rejoice and exult and give God the glory. Rev. 19:5-7

498. Pastor: Worship God with me, and let us exalt God's name together.
Congregation: Hallelujah! Let us be glad and rejoice!

499. Pastor: Be exalted, O God, above the heavens. Let your glory be over all the earth.

Congregation: Hallelujah! Let us be glad and rejoice. Let the people praise you, O God. Let all the people praise you. from Ps. 57,67

Prayers of Adoration

500. Holy, holy, holy, Lord God of hosts,
Heaven and earth are full of your glory.
Glory be to you, O Lord most high. Amen

501. Worthy are you, O God, to receive glory and honor and power; for you created all things and by your will they were created and existed. Great and wonderful are your deeds. Just and true are your ways. O Ruler of the ages, we stand in awe and glorify your name. You alone are holy. To you be blessing and honor and glory and might forever and ever. Amen.

502. Eternal God, the same yesterday, today and forever, you are glorious in grace full of love and compassion, abounding in grace and truth. All your works praise you in all places and at all times. We worship you. Praise be to you, O God. Amen.

503. Almighty God, the creator of all life and being, the fount of all goodness and beauty, the source of truth and love, hallowed be your name. To you be dominion, power, and glory forever and ever. Amen.

504. Pastor: Be exalted, O God, above the heavens. Let your glory be over all the earth.

Congregation: Hallelujah! Let us be glad and rejoice! Let the peoples praise you O God. Let all the peoples praise you. from Ps. 57, 67

Prayers of Confession

505. Confession in unison: O Spirit of God, who speaks to our spirits, created in your likeness, penetrate the depths of our being, the very springs of our personality. There cleanse and forgive us, we pray. Make us holy by your holiness, that so sanctified we may live the very life of Christ Jesus our Lord.

506. Creator God, bless us with a deep sense of your presence with us in this hour. We come to celebrate the beauty of your good earth, glorious blue skies, gardens overflowing with color, and long, soft summer days. O God, giver of every good gift, we have received from you a wealth of graciousness. Yet we confess the forgetfulness that fails to give thanks; the pride of ownership that is reluctant to share; the grasping for more, even when we have enough. Guide, forgive, and renew us, we pray, in the name of Jesus, the Christ. Amen.

507. Unison Prayer of Confession: Loving God, we realize we have not always made our homes the dwelling place of your love that we would like. Too often we act like individuals who happen to share the same building, rather than family members who care for one another. Help us to show our love and helpfulness in ways that reflect the kind of love you have shown us.

508. God of mercy and of hope, we confess that we come with mixed thoughts and uncertain dreams. We are offended by slight offenses or oversights against us and hardly consider our neglect of your Word, our patience with evil, and our slowness to act for others. We have not allowed our habits and perceptions to be transfigured by the glory of your grace and presence. We have forgotten the power of your promises to us. Help us. Heal us. Change us, O God. Amen.

509. Prayer of Confession (Unison): Lord, lead us to the empty tomb. Let us know that you are greater than the greatness of our sin. Then lead us back to our homes, our schools, our work places, assured that in the power of your forgiveness, change is possible. Set our sights on eternal life, so that we might fully love life on earth. In the name of the one who conquered death through death. Amen.

Prayer Before Offering

510. Creator of the visible and invisible divine deliverer, life-sustaining Spirit, all that is depends on you and rejoices in your praise. Thank you for your blessings and forgiveness. Enable us to give to you glory and receive us in your name. Amen.

511. Have a lay person give the offertory prayer (more apt to ask for sacrificial giving), but before prayer say something about his/her activities and/or position in church life.

Prayer Before Scripture

512. God of truth, who desires that we live by your truth, may the words spoken this day take root within the hearts of all who hear and be brought to fruition in true servanthood in the world. Amen.

513. Creator God, who commanded the light to shine out of darkness, through your Word enter into our hearts, that we may become for you lights in the world. Amen.

514. May the words of my mouth and the meditations of our hearts be acceptable to you, our rock and our redeemer. Amen.

515. Spirit of Truth, as we turn to your Word let the light of your consciousness be upon us, that we may come to know more fully the One who is the way, the truth, and the life, even Christ Jesus, our Lord. Amen.

516. Eternal God, take the human words which are about to be spoken and make of them a fitting channel for your holy Word.

The Lord's Prayer

517. Call it "The Prayer the Lord Taught His Disciples."

518. In the bulletin or announcement: In the Lord's Prayer we use "debts" and "debtors."

519. Have the Lord's Prayer sung by a soloist.

520. Have the Lord's Prayer sung by the congregation.

521. Give the Lord's Prayer in different languages.

522. Print entire version in bulletin or on screen.

523. Leader prays first part, with congregation joining in with "For Thine is the Kingdom, and the Power and the Glory for ever and ever. Amen."

524. Have a different salutation:

a. "Our Father, Creator, who art..."
b. "Gracious Parent, who are..."
c. "Our Father/Mother/Creator, who art..."
d. "Our Father and Mother God..."

525. An expanded translation from the Aramaic—

"Our Creator who is everywhere
May your name be sacred,
May your will be throughout the earth
Even as it is throughout the universe,
Provide us bread for our needs from day to day.
Forgive us our offenses even as we forgive our offenders
Let us not enter into possessiveness,
But separate us from evil,
Because you rule creation with the power
and the song, and the praise.
From all ages, throughout all ages
Sealed in faith, trust and truth. Amen."

CHAPTER 13

Music

Music plays a more important part of the worship service than is usually realized. Music can be uplifting spiritually. A song may touch people in a way a sermon can't. If worship is a celebration, the style of music should be upbeat, bright and joyful (Ps. 100:2). If music is well done, the worshippers do not notice the leader or the musicians, but instead, notice Jesus, the object of worship. The responsibility is to lead the congregation into His presence.This is not true when musicians concentrate on performance, talent, or personal recognition. In a few churches I visited the pianist/organist during the offering was more like a concert than an offertory accompaniment.

Some churches do not use musical instruments; and it is amazing how well they can stay on key. Of the dozen or more churches of this particular denomination even in small number of worshippers there was always someone able to lead singing without piano, organ, or other instruments.

MUSIC

Introduction

526. Have a member compose a welcome song for visitors using a familiar tune.

527. Have a "Hymn of the Month" and sing it each Sunday of the month.

528. Have a "Favorite Hymn Sunday" each quarter.

529. For smaller congregations have recorded songs with singers.

530. Instead of piano or organ, have guitar accompanying singing.

531. Instead of throwing away the old hymnals, take selected hymns and have them bound to keep or give away..

Congregational Singing

532. Instead of song leaders, call them "Praise Team", or "Worship Team."

533. Word of encouragement, "God has given you a voice. He has given you vocal chords. You may not have the voice of an angel, but God expects you to use it to His glory."

534. Word of encouragement, "If you don't sing well, sing loud. Make a joyful noise unto the Lord."

535. Encourage everyone to stand up and sing a wake-up song.

536. Begin the service with *This Is the Day the Lord Hath Made.*

537. If several songs, change song leaders every two or three songs.

538. In announcing the number of the hymn, while congregation is finding it in the hymnals, read the first verse, or say something about the hymn or author.

539. On a familiar song, have soloist begin, then congregation joins in.

540. Or say, "When you find the number in the hymnal say, 'Praise the Lord'. If you have not yet found it say, 'Hold on, Preacher'."

541. Have different members of the worship team introduce the hymns with Scripture or other comments.

542. Use deaf signs on songs as *Lord, I Lift Your Name on High.*

543. On the first verse, full volume; Second verse, bring it down; Third verse, lower; Fourth verse, full volume.

544. Increase tempo with each stanza on selected songs.

545. Have brass ensemble play the next to last verse.

546. Instead of singing the usual 1, 2, and 5 verses, sing verses 3 and 4 after reading them.

547. Sing the third verse of several songs, and have "Ode to the Third Stanza" printed in the bulletin:

Ode to the Third Stanza
by David A. Robb
(used with permission)

I think that I shall never see
a resurrected stanza three;
The third, with oft the salient thought
revealing why the hymn was wrought;
The third, which sometimes bares the soul
the hymnist wanted seen as whole;
The third, replace by interlude
through which we stand in somber mood;
"Let's sing the first, the second and last,"
the way we've done it in the past!"
Hymns are sung by folk like me,
but only God sings stanza three!

548. In hymns with four stanzas have soloist sing the third, then all join again on the last.

549. Where there is a pause in the verse or refrain followed by a significant statement of faith, the leader says, "Believe it," or "You know," or "Sing it."

550. After each song have a short prayer (talk with God), testimony, or Scripture.

551. On hymns with the word "stand" or "standing", as in *Stand Up; Stand Up for Jesus*, or *Standing on the Promises of God* everyone stands when those words are sung.

552. In a bilingual service have the hymns sung simultaneously in English and another language.

553. To introduce a new song, have the pianist or organist play single notes.

554. Sing the last verse of the hymn a cappella.

555. If singing gets tiresome have all sing first verse, women on second, men on third, and all on fourth.

556. When clapping is allowed or encouraged, vary the rhythm of the clapping to fit the song. Example, "He Lives" (clap, clap), "He Lives" (clap, clap), wherever there is a pause in the song.

557. Sing the last verse slower, then pick up the tempo with the chorus.

558. For hymns where the congregation is scheduled to stand, the organist/pianist plays the tune softer than usual, then changes volume for the signal for the congregation to stand.

559. Sing one verse of the hymn, then pastor quotes a complementary Scripture. Same with other verses.

560. Sing three verses seated, then pianist plays chorus while worshippers stand for the last verse.

561. In songs with pauses, have echo (men, women, choir), Example, the refrains

a. *It Is Well With My Soul*
b. *There Is Power In the Blood*
c. *When the Roll Is Called Up Yonder*

562. Bulletin announcement, "During the Song of Praise, those who would like to sing the beloved "Hallelujah Chorus" are invited to come forward by the side aisles, or follow the ushers as they come forward with the offering.

Music will be available at the front. After picking up the music, join the choirs in the chancel.

Choirs

563. Adult choirs, call them **Celebration Singers**.

564. Children's Choirs, call them
- a. **Sonbeams** (3 years through Kindergarten)
- b. **Joyful Sounds** (Grades 1-6)
- c. **Carpenter's Choir** (Grades 3-5)
- d. **Cornerstone Choir** (Grades 3-5)
- e. **Kingdom Kids Choir** (K-2nd Grade)
- f. **Rockin' Angels** (Grades 1-6)
- g. **Light Shine Choir** (6th through 8th Grades)

565. Forty-five minutes before the church service, schedule a Choir Warm-up.

566. In the bulletin: "We have a chair reserved for you in the choir loft."

567. Have choir rehearsal first Friday of the month and call it "Celebration Friday."

568. At choir practices have other members of the church rotate on refreshments.

569. Choir in balcony in back, not seen.

570. Choir enters before the minister, remains standing, then sits when pastor sits.

571. Choir processional from the back, slow step with beat of music remaining standing in aisle(s) for the singing of the first song.

572. On one Sunday have the choir members go down to congregation during the service and randomly select worshippers to join them in special music.

575. If choir is on vacation during summer have members sit sparingly in the congregation listening for potential choir members.

576. If choir members take their places with the congregation after the anthem, they stand until all are in position and then sit down together.

577. Have the choir (quartet, trio, duet, or solo) sing the verse and have the congregation sing the chorus that is printed in the bulletin.

578. After the summer vacation have a choir welcome back dinner party for all choir members and new ones.

CHAPTER 14

Offering

The offering is not just a collection but an act of worship. If more people would realize that, the offerings would increase.

It is well for a church to inform visitors that they are not expected to put anything in the offering plate; though at one church I visited the pastor of this large church announced that every Sunday they had visitors, people who were just passing through. He then told them when the offering plate came by, don't let it pass without putting something in it.

Some churches require their members to tithe or contribute financially or they lose their membership. A contribution statement is their certificate of membership. In one church all the tithers were asked to come to the front with their tithes; and after they returned to their seats, the others were asked to go forward to give their offerings. This was not an idea for this book, though it is a fresh one from my point of view. Another idea not in the book was given to me by a friend from Sri Lanki (Ceylon). The churches in that country give the Christmas offering to the pastor and the Easter offering to the assistant pastor.

OFFERING

General

579. Call it "God's Tithes and Our Offerings"

580. Call it "Member Giving"

581. Call it "Give-Back-To-God Portion"

582. Encourage children at an early age to give to the Lord.

583. Don't ask the people for money—always ask the Lord.

584. Instead of asking for a specific amount from members, ask them to tithe without stating the amount.

585. Have the ushers seated in front to save time.

586. Have automatic tithing arrangement with the members' banks to be charged to their checking accounts.

587. Instead of flat offering plates use receptacle deep enough to maintain privacy of the giver.

588. Have two plates—one for general expenses and a wicker basket for the needy.

589. Have the offering plates/baskets in back for worshippers to give after the service.

590. Designate all coins in the offering plate to go to Women's Ministry to keep the House of God in order.

591. Have a family (father, mother, son, daughter) take up the offering, and list their names in the bulletin.

592. At the beginning of the new year mail letters to members and other contributors giving a tax deductible contribution statement to the church for the past year.

593. On the Commitment Card have a chart showing the approximate weekly gift proportionate to income.

594. Have a card not to be construed as a contract but intention of commitment.

595. Have a note, "This commitment may be increased or decreased or canceled due to changing circumstances by notifying the treasurer."

596. On the commitment card for checking ☐ I am a tither and I will now step up from God's minimum to ____% and estimate my gifts to average$________per week. Signed____________________.

597. Collect attendance cards separately from the offering.

598. Consider the policy of one church, "Taking a public offering is not our solution to financing the organizational structure of our church. That is important to remember. The central reason for taking a public offering is the tactile symbolism it affords us. It gives us a chance to concretely offer up to God the fruit of our labor, our value, our wealth, our pleasure, our source of livelihood. Much as an earlier agrarian culture might offer up apples, or corn, or tomatoes, we write a check. It gives us opportunity to go beyond "offering" as a concept and allows us one tangible memorable identifiable mark that indeed we are trying to learn what it means to offer all that we are to God."

599. Comments Before Offering

a. God has the cattle on a thousand hills—all He needs is cowboys to round them up. Will the ushers come forward for the offering? (This could be more productive if the ushers dressed as cowboys).

b. Your faith gets a real test when you find yourself in church with nothing less than a twenty dollar bill, and it's funny how a twenty dollar bill can seem so small at the grocery store and so big at church.

c. A generous person forgets what he gives and remembers what he receives.

d. It is not how much of OUR money we should give to God, but how much of GOD'S money we should keep for ourselves.

e. God loveth a cheerful giver—don't be like the miser who prayed, 'Lord, you can have anything you can pry out of my hands'.

f. Now let us return to the Lord the portion due unto Him according to that which we reported on Form 1040, line 23.

g. Some give until it hurts. We hope you are not sensitive to pain.

h. Tithing is not $^1/_{10}$ th of what you ought to give.

i. Our offerings are given in response to the many blessings that have come from our gracious and loving God. Offering boxes have been place in the narthex near each inside door. You may place your offerings there either at the beginning or close of each service. Children are encouraged to begin this practice at a very early age.

j. A word about our offering. Our offering is not a collection of money. It is a privilege for those who believe in the Lord Jesus Christ and are baptized into His family to return a portion of the gifts we have received from Him. We respond to His love with our offerings to build His church and to reach out with His saving Gospel. This congregation has committed to supporting the ministry of the Gospel here and around the world through our offerings. We ask that our visitors should not feel obligated to give an offering today.

k. Our Unified Budget is based on faith giving, not on a pledge system. Your contributions to our church are private between you and God (and the financial secretary for recording purposes only.)

l. The Lord loveth a cheerful giver. He also accepteth from a grouch.

m. The Lord loveth a cheerful giver—until he brags about it.

n. Support the church with your money. You can't take it with you, but you can send it on ahead.

o. Don't give till it hurts—Give till it feels good.

p. Give not from the top of your purse, but from the bottom of your heart.

q. Giving is the thermometer of our love.

r. The world is composed of givers and takers. The takers may eat better, but the givers sleep better.

s. It is O.K. if you take the attitude of the old lady who said, "Pastor, I don't see how I can give as much as a tenth. Would it be all right if I give a fourth?"

600. Scripture Before Offering

a. *"Give liberally and be ungrudging when you do so, for on this account God will bless you in all your work and in all that you undertake."* Deut. 15:10

b. *"Open your hand to the poor and needy neighbor in your land."* Deut. 15:11

c. *"All shall give as they are able, according to the blessing of God that has been given to you."* Deut. 16:17

d. *"Ascribe to God glory! Bring an offering, and come into God's courts."* Ps. 96:8

e. *"Honor God with your substance and with the first fruits of all your produce."* Prov. 3:9

f. *"Bring the full tithe into the storehouse."* Mal. 3:10

g. *"When you are offering your gift at the altar, if you remember that your brother or sister has something against you, leave your gift there before the altar and go, first be reconciled to your brother or sister, and then come and offer your gift. "* Matt. 5:23-24

h. *"Do not store up for yourselves treasures on earth, where moth and rust consume and where thieves break in and steal; but store up for yourselves treasures in heaven, where neither moth nor rust consumes and where thieves do not break in and steal. For where your treasure is, there will your heart be also."* Matt. 6:19-21

i. *"Freely you have received, freely give."* Matt. 10:8

j. *"Give to the emperor the things that are the emperor's and to God the things that are God's."* Matt. 22:21

k. *"From everyone to whom much has been given, much will be required; and from the one to whom much has been entrusted, even more will be demanded."* Luke 12:48

l. *"Whoever is faithful in a very little is faithful also in much. No one can serve two masters. You cannot serve God and wealth."* Luke 16:10,13

m. *"Remember the words of the Lord Jesus, for He Himself said, 'It is more blessed to give than to receive.'"* Acts 20:35

n. *"It is required of stewards that they be found trustworthy."* I Cor. 4:2

o. "*On the first day of every week, each of you is to put something aside and store it up, as you may prosper."* I Cor. 16:2

p. "*Each of you must give as you have made up your mind, not reluctantly or under compulsion, for God loves a cheerful giver."* I Cor. 9:7

q. *"Do not neglect to do good and to share what you have, for such sacrifices are pleasing to God."* Heb. 13:16

601. Prayer Before Offering

a. O God, through the offerings of these gifts may we become a more open people, open-minded in hearing your Word, open-hearted in healing a broken world, open-handed in heeding your call for charity. With thanks for all good gifts, we present a portion of our substance and the whole of ourselves. Amen

b. Blessed are you, O Lord, our God, maker of all things. Through your goodness you have blessed us with these gifts. With them we offer ourselves to your service and dedicate our lives to the care and redemption of all that you have made, for the sake of Him Who gave Himself for us, Jesus Christ our Lord. Amen

b. Blessed are you, O Lord, our God, maker of all things. Through your goodness you have blessed us with these gifts. With them we offer ourselves to your service and dedicate our lives to the care and redemption of all that you have made, for the sake of Him Who gave Himself for us, Jesus Christ our Lord. Amen

c. Create in me a clean heart, O God, and renew a right spirit within me. Cast me not away from thy presence, and take not thy Holy Spirit from me. Restore unto me the joy of thy salvation, and uphold me with thy free spirit. Amen.

d. Gracious God, from whom all good things come, we give you thanks for creating us, for sustaining us with grace, for redeeming us through your love, and for making us partners in your kingdom. Help us to be thankful for all your gifts. May all people share in the bounty of your love through these offerings. Amen

e. Teach us, God, to serve you as you deserve; to give and not to count the cost; to labor and not ask for reward; save in the knowledge that we do your will.

f. We give but little when we give our possessions. It is when we giver ourselves that we truly give.

During the Offering

602. The pastor sets the example after the offertory prayer of reaching into his pocket and placing his envelope in the offering.

603. During the offering the organist or pianist plays a lively tune, not too loud, not too showy, not too long.

604. Have a big basket in front. Worshippers go down center aisle, give offering, kneel at the altar if they wish, return at the outside aisles.

605. During the offering have a skit about a coming event.

606. If attendance is low, ushers shake hands with each worshipper before handing him/her the plate.

607. During the offering have slides or video of church, members, activities, camps, etc. but not to be a distraction from giving.

608. After the offering hold the Bible high and sing an appropriate and familiar song.

Special Fund Raising Ideas

609. Have a Change Bottle or Box in each home. Every night family members empty pockets of all coins. At the end of certain period each family goes to the front on a specified Sunday and empties their bottle in a 5-gallon water bottle. Congregation applauds with each donation. Each family does not count the money.

610. Have a "Pennies From Heaven" jar for World Hunger at back of church.

611. In the narthex have an empty 5-gallon water bottle labeled "People of Change".

612. Have a book sale once a year for members to bring books they no longer need and sell cheaply.

613. Have a "SPUD NIGHT' fund raiser featuring baked potatoes with various toppings, salads and ice cream with toppings.

614. Have a quilt show and craft boutique and charge $20 (?) per table.

615. Have a live auction for such items as a dinner, resort, show, ball game, cruise, airline mileage, entertainment, automobile (anything above dealer cost), hotel package, etc.

616. Have a T-shirt sale.

617. Have a Parking Lot sale with all members and others bringing articles to sell. Advertise BYOB (Bring Your Own Bag).

618. Have a fishbowl in the narthex with donations going to help defray the cost of sending the church's delegate to District and General Conferences.

619. At the beginning of football season or at the Super Bowl have picture of football with goal posts, motto, slogan, and financial goal.

620. Have an Annual Souper Supper at the beginning of Stewardship Sunday or the Super Bowl.

621. Offer members the opportunity to give monetary gifts in memory of a friend or loved one. These gifts are a wonderful way to honor one who has died and to advance the work of the Lord as well. Acknowledgments of memorial gifts are sent to the donor and the bereaved family. List in the bulletin the gifts recently received in memory of loved ones.

622. The pastor says, "I am sure it is no secret to this audience that we are in a fund-raising campaign—and that means YOU are in a fund-raising campaign. I have prepared three sermons for this morning. What I call my Ten Dollar Sermon last one full hour. My Fifty Dollar Sermon lasts 30 minutes. My One Hundred Dollar Sermon lasts only fifteen minutes. We will now pass the collection plate and see which sermon I deliver."

CHAPTER 15

Scripture Reading

If the Scripture reading is the same Sunday after Sunday, it can become perfunctory. The ideas in this chapter are intended to make Scripture reading more meaningful, with more member participation.

If pew Bibles are used, the pastor should tell the worshippers the page number of the Scripture reading. Doing so prevents some attendees from being embarrassed.

After I assembled the 1001 ideas for this book, one idea came to me which may indeed be a fresh idea for all of the 500 churches visited, and, as far as I know, for the countless churches not visited. The idea is concerned with the memorization of Scripture. In Sunday School students recite verses or passages of Scripture and give the reference. If this were done in a worship service connecting the Scripture to its reference, memorization would be easier. In this book are examples for the pastor to give the references after reading the Scripture and also for the congregation to give references in responsive readings.

(1) Scriptural Calls to Worship—Ideas 421 and 422
(2) Scriptures before the Offering—Idea 600
(3) Scriptures before the Altar Call—Ideas 683 to 687
(4) Scriptures before Dismissal—Ideas 719 to 722

Scripture Reading

623. In the bulletin, "All Scripture references are from the *New International Version* (NIV) unless otherwise noted. GN=*Good News For Modern Man,* NASB=*New American Standard Bible,* NCV=*New Century Version,* NLT=*New Living Translation,* JB=*Jerusalem Bible,* PH=*Phillips,* TM=*The Message,* KJV=*King James Version*

624. Leader reads from same version as in the pew racks.

625. In the worship bulletin list page of the pew rack Bibles.

626. Have the Scripture on overhead screen.

627. Have the Scripture in the bulletin insert.

628. For Christmas have the Christmas story (Luke 2:8-20) printed in the bulletin insert in different versions while the pastor reads from the King James Version.

629. Have all stand for the reading of the Scripture.

630. For the text-verse have all worshippers read with pastor after he says, "Let's fill the house of the Lord with the Word of the Lord."

631. Pastor, "We are here to DIGEST Scripture—and not to go away with inDIGESTion."

632. If the Scripture reading is short, read it in different versions or have different people reading each version.

633. If the Scripture reading is long, have a stopping point with special music, then finish the Scripture reading.

634. Have the Scripture reading from the back (unseen).

635. Slowly read the KJV and worshippers follow with another version.

636. Pastor, "While you are Bible shuffling, I'll give some background for the Scripture."

637. Pastor, "If you have found the Scripture say 'Praise the Lord!' If you have not found it, say, 'Hold On, Preacher'."

638. Pastor (reader) comes to the congregation halfway down the center aisle and the worshippers stand and face the pastor.

639. Have a young person lead in the responsive reading.

640. Have different members of the church Board read the Scriptures.

641. Have different members read portions of the Scripture (plan ahead).

642. Have someone who had a perfect Sunday School attendance record read the Scripture.

643. Pastor announces the Scripture reader for the following Sunday. (Pastor may use that as an excuse to call on the family to hear practice and to help them understand the Scripture to be read.)

644. Before reading the Scripture, especially the parables, tell it in your own words.

645. If more than one minister, have all read the Scripture in unison.

646. Read the Scripture (or memorize it if short) by a family in unison.

647. Have families, or couples, or Sunday School class go forward and sit in the front to give the Scripture reading.

648. After the Scripture reading, the reader says, *"This is the Word of the Lord."* Then the people respond, *"Thanks be to God."*

649. After the Scripture reading, "May the Lord add His blessing to the reading and to THE HEARING of His Word."

CHAPTER 16

Childrens Sermons

Keep in mind that the attention span of a child is usually correlated to his or her age.

If children's response to questions asked are not heard by the congregation, the story teller repeats their answers.

This chapter has suggestions related to the children's sermon, other names, and conclusion.

Sermons for Children

Preparation

650. If no carpet in front, have sample carpet pads for kids to sit on.

651. Have microphone available for children's responses so audience can hear them.

652. Make them feel comfortable and ask a lot of questions (Art Linkletter style).

653. Coordinate children's sermon with Sunday School lesson.

654. Coordinate children's sermon with the pastor's sermon.

655. Coordinate children's sermon to holidays or other special days of the year.

656. If any members are good story tellers, let them give the Children's Sermon.

657. Have offering taken before Children's Sermon so children can learn about giving.

658. Have the organist/pianist play *Jesus Loves the Little Children* as the children go forward.

Children's Church Bulletin Notices

659. Call the bulletin by another name—

a. *Children's Chat*
b. *Children's Message*
c. *Children's Moment*
d. *Children's Sermonette*
e. *Time With Our Children*
f. *Younger Story Lovers*

660. As soon as congregation starts singing #_______, all children ages 3-12 are invited to come forward for a short children's message. Parents may accompany them if they wish.

661. Visiting children are always welcome.

Concluding the Children's Sermon

662. At the end of the children's sermon, pastor says "Now, let's talk to God."

663. After the children's sermon, pastor says a prayer of petitions with children repeating after each petition.

664. Announce, "Time for the children to have their own service."

665. Announce on screen, "Children in Preschool and grades 1-6 please go to the Children's Church"

666. Pastor, "Let us continue worship all over the building."

667. Pastor, "Following the Children's Message, children are invited to participate in a children's choir or other activities. Of course, children and youth are always welcome to participate in the worship service and may remain for the entire service if they wish."

CHAPTER 17

Sermons

In a recent survey it was found that the pastor's sermon had the most influence on whether or not visitors would return. Loyal members may return if the message is mediocre, but visitors were less likely to be persuaded to come back.

My observance showed that few pastors can read their sermons effectively. There were some sermons that had me thinking that "sermons that are read are like flowers that are dead."

This chapter is not one on homiletics—there are numerous books on the subject; but some of the ideas here may be new.

Most of the sermons I heard in the 500+ churches visited were messages of hope; but some seemed to beat up rather than lift up. Early generations heard more sermons of condemnation that the 21st Century worshiper wants.

One idea not on the original list is: At the beginning of the year have the members indicate what they want the pastor to preach on in the coming year. In one such survey 70% of the membership requested messages on the *Book of Revelation.*

The Sermon

668. Instead of calling it “Sermon”, call it “Word In Dialogue”

669. Instead of “Sermon”, call it “Message”.

670. Have the main points of the sermon in the bulletin insert, with the Scripture.

671. If the sermon is delivered without notes, stories told are read from a card.

672. Have the sermon related to a daily devotion from the past week, or ask members which devotional they would like to have in a sermon.

673. If the sermon is not interesting, people may think that God is uninteresting.

674. The way to preach interesting sermons is to be an interesting person.

675. Preachers should listen to their own sermons.

676. Sermons should present good news rather than bad news.

677. In advertising, try to use sermon titles that will attract the un-churched.

678. Before the sermon sing *Open My Eyes That I MaySee.*

679. On a hot day get the attention of the audience by saying “Today I am going to be bold, be brief, and be seated.”

680. Have a five-minute message for the teenagers.

681. After making an essential point say, “Turn to your neighbor and say ‘That’s right’.”

682. In smaller churches, open for discussion after the sermon.

CHAPTER 18

The Altar Call

The altar call may well be the most important part of the worship service. It is encouraging to find churches that still have a hymn of invitation for the unsaved to publicly profess faith in Jesus Christ.

This chapter attempts to show the importance of the altar call, but that evangelism does not stop there. The list of Scripture readings here is not complete. Perhaps church members can add to the list.

Altar Call

Scripture Before Altar Call

683. *Jesus said, "Come to me, all you that are weary and carrying heavy burdens, and I will give you rest."* Matthew 11:28

684. *"Since we are justified by faith, we have peace with God through Jesus Christ. There is therefore no condemnation for those who are in Christ."* Romans 5:1; 8:1

685. *"The saying is sure and worthy of full acceptance, that Christ Jesus came into the world to save sinners."* I Timothy 1:15

686. *"This is the message we have heard from God and proclaim to you, that God is light and in God there is no darkness at all. If we walk in the light as God is light, we have fellowship with one another, and the blood of Jesus cleanses us from all sin."* I John 1:5,7

687. We Care About You! (Name)________Church wants you to have the abundant life. We want you to:

1. Realize your need for Christ. The Bible teaches that all are sinners and that the result of sin is death and separation from God. Rom. 3:23; 6:23

2. Acknowledge Christ's death and resurrection. Jesus received our sin, died in our place and then conquered death so that we could have an abundant, eternal life. 2 Cor. 5:21; Rom. 10:9

3. Turn from self and let Christ come into your life as Lord and Savior. You can give yourself to Jesus and invite the Spirit into your life. Luke 9:23; John 1:12

Procedure

688. On the first verse of the invitational hymn ask those who wish to transfer membership come forward. On the second verse ask those who wish to re-dedicate their lives come forward. On the third verse ask all those who wish to accept Christ come forward, and on the fourth verse ask all those who wish to know more about accepting Christ come forward.

689. Have the invitation the same time as communion service.

690. Before the altar call give a Scripture and comment.

691. Have the prayer team go to front when the invitation is given.

692. Have the invitational hymn related to the sermon.

693. For those going forward to accept Christ give them a Bible or a film on Jesus.

694. In larger churches ask trained counselors and prayer partners to come to the front to talk with those desiring salvation, rededication, or church membership. (Strangers should be directed to the pastor.)

Invitation

695. Any person desiring to make a commitment to Jesus Christ or to join the church by baptism, by transfer of membership, or by Christian experience is invited to come forward and be greeted.

696. If you've not made the wonderful discovery of a personal relationship with Jesus Christ, we invite you to speak with our pastor or an elder after the service or pick up a booklet in the pew rack or Narthex entitled, "Steps to Peace With God." Don't let another day go by without the assurance of knowing you belong to Him.

697. With all standing and eyes closed, if you are shy or fearful, ask the person next to you to go down the aisle with you.

698. With all eyes closed, if you have a need, I will pray for you—You don't need to come forward, just raise your hand and put it down.

699. With eyes closed, settle with God, then come forward.

700. All heads bowed and eyes closed—raise your hand if you are sure you would go to heaven if you died right now.

701. If you would like to know more about how to become a Christian, simply make a note on the Silent Roll card enclosed in your program folder.

702. Raise your hand if you are ready....Raise hand if you will give it a second thought.

703. With all heads bowed, look up if you wish to make a decision for Christ.

704. May the only movement be someone coming forward.

705. As you leave this service, if the Holy Spirit is speaking to you, you may not sleep until it is settled.

706. We will sing one more verse—it's worth waiting for. I feel there is a young lady here today whose life needs to be turned around.

CHAPTER 19

Closing and Follow-up

When expressing appreciation to the visitors and inviting them to return, don't forget to do the same for the regular attenders. Most churches have the same way of closing a worship service. This chapter suggests different ways which may be refreshing to the regular worshippers.

Included are some Scriptural dismissals and responsive dismissals; and the church members may be challenged to find more.

I estimated that 95% of the churches I visited followed up with a letter from the pastor, usually a form letter and rather impersonal. But there were a few hand-written letters (from the pastor or a member) which made a much greater impression.

Closing and Followup

707. Have congregation remain seated during postlude.

708. For a closing song have a lively song as *Shine, Jesus, Shine*, or *Celebrate.*

709. At the end of the service have all worshippers form circle around sanctuary, hold hands and sing a farewell song.

710. Instead of a closing hymn, have a hymn of departure, or hymn of commitment

711. At end of service have different worshippers respond briefly to the sermon.

712. At close of service have choir go to back singing, *God Be With You.*

713. At close of service have flashed on screen the name of the church and "**Thank You For Joining Us**."

714. At the close, the worshippers remain seated, pastor goes to first row which stands and in departing each is greeted by the pastor. This is followed by each row.

715. Pastor goes to back of sanctuary, asks the congregation to fix eyes on the cross as pastor comments or quotes a Scripture about the cross. Then he dismisses the congregation.

716. Have the worship leaders exit before the rest of the congregation.

717. Have a recycling bin for bulletins.

718. After the service have a "Coffee and Conversation" time.

The Dismissal

719. "*God will keep your going out and coming in from this time on and forevermore.* Amen." Psalm 121:8

720. *"The grace of Jesus Christ, the love of God, and the communion of the Holy Spirit be with all of you."* Amen. II Corinthians 13:14

721. *"Now to our God, who by the power at work within us is able to accomplish abundantly far more than all we ask or imagine, to God be glory in the church and in Christ Jesus to all generations, forever and ever.* Amen." Ephesians 3:20-21

722. *"Beloved, whatever is true, whatever is honorable, whatever is just, whatever is pure, whatever is pleasing, whatever is commendable, if there is any excellence and if there is anything worthy of praise, think about these things. Keep on doing the things that you have learned and received and heard and seen in me, and the God of peace will be with you.* Amen." Philippians 4:8-9

723. *"May you be filled with the knowledge of God's will in all spiritual wisdom and understanding, so that you may lead lives worthy of God.* Amen." Colossians 1:9-10

724. "Gracious God, as we depart from this place of worship we pray that you will make us instruments of your peace; where there is hatred, let us sow love; where there is injury, pardon; where there is doubt, faith; where there is despair, hope; where there is darkness, light; and where there is sadness, comfort. Amen." Francis of Assisi (adapted)

725. "Loving God, as we go from worship into the world, grant that we may not so much seek to be consoled as to console; to be understood, as to understand; to be loved, as to love; for it is in giving that we receive; It is in pardoning that we are pardoned, and it is in dying that we are born to eternal life. Amen." Francis of Assisi (adapted)

726. "May Christ be near you to defend you, within you to refresh you, around you to preserve you, before you to guide you, behind you to justify you, above you to bless you. Amen." Latin Prayer, Tenth Century

727. Pastor: "Our service of worship now ends, Our worship through service now begins."

728. "*God bless you and keep you;*
God's face shine upon you and be gracious to you;
God look upon you with love and give you peace. Amen."
Numbers 6:24-26

729. Go in peace, so you may be a calming influence at home, at work, at school,
Go in joy, so you may brighten every corner you enter;
Go in hope, so you may encourage all those around you;
Go in faith, so you may point others to Christ.

730. *"Now the God of peace, that brought again from the dead our Lord Jesus, that great shepard of the sheep, through the blood of the everlasting covenant, Make you perfect in every good work to do his will, working in you that which is wellpleasing in his sight, through Jesus Christ; to whom be glory for ever and ever. Amen."* KJV Hebrews 13:20-21

731. "As those who wait for the second coming with a living hope, through the resurrection of Jesus Christ from the dead, may we live our lives rejoicing with joy inexpressible and full of glory—to the praise and glory and honor of Jesus Christ, because we love Him and we long for the day that we will live with Him. Amen. "

732. Responsive Dismissals

a. **Pastor**: Go in Peace. Serve the Lord.
People: Thanks be to God.

b. **Pastor**: According to the riches of His glory, God grant that you may be strengthened in your inner being with power through His Spirit, and that Christ may dwell in your hearts through faith, as you are being rooted and grounded in love. May you have the power to comprehend, with all the saints, what is the breadth and length and height and depth, and to know the love of Christ that surpasses knowledge, so that you may be filled with all the fullness of God.
People: Now to Him Who by the power that works within us is able to accomplish abundantly far more than all we can ask or imagine, to Him be glory in the church and in Christ Jesus to all generations, forever and ever. Amen.

c. **Pastor**: "N*ow may the God of peace, who brought again from the dead our Lord Jesus Christ, the great Shepherd of the sheep, through the blood of the everlasting covenant—make you perfect in every good work to do His will working in you that which is well-pleasing in His sight; through Jesus Christ, to whom be glory forever and ever."* Hebrews 13:20-21
People: Amen.

d. **Pastor**: Let the peace of Christ rule in your hearts since as members of one body you were called to peace. Be thankful.
People: Amen. Amen. Let it be so.

e. **Pastor**: *"May the God of steadfastness and encouragement grant you to live in harmony with one another in accordance with Christ Jesus."* Romans 15:5
People: Amen.

f. **Pastor**: Jesus Christ is the sun of righteousness. May His radiance bring you warmth and cheer.
People: Amen.

g. **Pastor:** Light and peace are yours through Jesus Christ. May your light so shine before others that they see your works and glorify your Father in heaven.
People: Amen.

h. **Pastor:** Almighty God, Father, Son, and Holy Spirit, bless you now and forever.
People: Amen.

Followup

733. Within three days have the lay people call on visitors on behalf of the pastor.

734. Train the visitor to go in pairs: what to say, and what not to say (as "See you in church Sunday", or "Why did you visit our church?")

735. Have a Cookie Patrol, leave cookies with note.

736. Encourage small group members to visit by couples. Leave home-baked bread or cookies, but do not go in. If invited, say "We don't want to interrupt your day."

737. Encourage young people to do visitation.

738. Invite visitors to a free lunch to know more about the church or the Christian life.

739. Mail postcard with picture of church, address and message in good handwriting.

740. If the followup is by letter, make it short and reasonable and personal (not a form letter). Remember something about the visitor, home, state, city, guest of ___________, etc.

741. Enclose a self addressed stamped postcard for their comments about their visit—ratings on friendliness, music, preaching, facilities, etc. and place for suggestions.

742. Make your facilities available to outside groups that include your members—The object is evangelism.

743. Use your church for a polling place on Election Day. Have home-made cookies and coffee, etc. Have tracts available about salvation, but nothing about your church.

744. Have a "Clothes Closet" for new and good used clothing for the needy. Make it a news item (free advertising for the church).

745. Have a "Stork Exchange"—a variety of infant to toddler items for the needy. (Another news item.)

746. Have a "Flea market" for a special cause.

747. Have a 10-minute video about the church and its programs and opportunities, using testimonials. This can be used before the worship service, given to visitors, or left in homes visited.

748. Have a card titled **"Ten Top Excuses Why People Don't Go To Church."**

10, Can't find a polyester leisure suit anywhere.
9, Relate to jazz and rock more than Handel and Bach.
8, Would rather sleep in own bed than in pew.
7, One word: HYPOCRITES.
6, Went all the time as a child.
5, I gave at the office.
4, During organ music, I start craving ballpark hot dogs.
3, Can remember only three Commandments.
2, Feel guilty already.
1. I'm too busy.

These are all **excuses.** Perhaps the **reason** why they don't go to church is because they have not attended (name of) Church.

749. Have a Pictorial Directory with a photographer taking pictures of each family. Arrange for no charge for the pictures for the directory, but the photographer charges for individual family pictures. These are taken under the church name and are displayed in the homes where visitors can see them.

750. Have a calendar with picture of church, pastor(s), missionaries supported, special events/projects for each month.

751. Have a one-page yearly calendar.

752. Have a Yearly Pocket Planner along the format of a commercial planner.

753. Have church business cards with church information, and on back map of location.

754. Have a business card with information on front and magnet on back.

755. Have an ad inviting readers to have a "spiritual oasis" by calling for a three-minute message.

756. Have a paid newspaper advertisement once a quarter (then the newspaper is apt to report news and print pictures.)

757. In ads, have the phone number of the church in large print and the pastor's name in smaller print.

758. Place your ad in the yellow pages or newspaper or flyers as **information** rather than **persuasion.**

759. Have mass mailing cards rather than letters.

760. Have mass mailings to target the unchurched to invite them to church rather than to accept Christ.

CHAPTER 20

The Holy Communion

Of the 500+ churches I visited most called this ordinance or sacrament "Communion" Other names are listed in this chapter.

Here we attempt to show how different churches approach Communion. Several ideas on the invitation to observe this act of worship are given. Many churches observe it every Sunday, others once a month, and a few once a year.

As to the ordinance/sacrament of Baptism I observed so few that I have only one idea to be included in this book. Pastor Gary, senior pastor of a growing church, follows the example of the Apostle Paul in that he himself does not baptize but has associates do it.

The Holy Communion

The Ordinance/Sacrament of Communion

761. Other names for the Ordinance/Sacrament of Communion
- **a.** The Lord's Supper
- **b.** The Lord's Table
- **c.** Holy Communion
- **d**. Eucharist
- **e.** Holy Eucharist
- **f.** The Table of the Lord
- **g**. The Table of God

762. Have a statement in the bulletin regarding communion and who participates.

763. Have a soloist sing an appropriate hymn/song while the elements are passed.

764. Each time read from a different version of the Bible and say which version.

765. Have members give a short communion meditation.

766. On the Sundays when Communion is served have two banners in front of the sanctuary **"This is My Body which is given for you. Do this in remembrance of Me,"** and **"This cup is the new covenant in My Blood which is shed for you."**

767. During preparation for Communion give congregation choice of standing, sitting, or kneeling.

768. Our Communion Statement: I believe that in Holy Communion, our Lord graciously shares His Body and Blood with us through bread and wine. He does this in order to forgive our sins, assure us of our salvation, strengthen us for Christian living, and unite us more closely as members of His family, the Church. Repenting of my sins, believing in the presence of Christ in this Sacrament, and re-dedicating my life to live according to His will, I announce my desire to receive Holy Communion.

769. Remind congregation that Jesus served ALL His disciples—Judas who betrayed Him, Peter who denied Him, Thomas who doubted Him, James and John who argued over top spot in the Kingdom.

770. COMMUNION helps us understand what Jesus did for us when He gave His life on the cross. The bread (or wafers) and grape juice (or wine) are emblems (or symbols) of Christ's body and blood, just as our country's flag is the emblem of America. When we see the flag, we remember the many persons who died so we could have freedom to worship God. So it is with communion which is sometimes called **The Lord's Supper**. Bread and a small cup of grape juice are common things, broken bread represents Christ's body, broken as the nails pierced His hands and feet and the spear pierced His side; the cup represents the blood that He shed for us.

771. The Lord's Supper is a time to *remember* the life, death and resurrection of Jesus. It is a time to *repent* of our sins. It is a time to *reconcile* with people from whom we have been alienated. It is a time to *renew* our devotion. It is a time to *rejoice* in having a personal covenant relationship with the one true living God.

772. A sacrament is the breaking through of the sacred into the profane; a ritual is the ceremonial acting out of the profane in order to show forth its sacredness. A sacrament is God offering holiness to people; a ritual is people raising up the holiness of their humanity to God.

773. We believe that the body and blood of Christ are truly present in and with the bread and wine when we receive the Sacrament. We do not believe that the bread and wine somehow mystically "change" into something other than bread and wine, nor do we believe that the bread and wine merely "represent" Christ's body and blood; rather, we are bound by the words of our Lord and Savior Jesus Christ when He said, *"Take, eat, this is my body,"* and *"Take, drink, this is my blood."* We believe and teach that when we receive the bread and wine, we are also truly receiving the body and blood of Christ (because of His divine words). We, therefore, also believe the Sacrament of Holy Communion is more than just a memorial, we believe it is Christ truly coming to us and offering His body and blood in an outward sign of His love for us and as an outward assurance of the forgiveness He won for us by His death on the Cross.

If you are able to accept our understanding of Holy Communion, you are cordially invited to partake of the Sacrament with us. However, if you are in doubt, you may wish to consult with the Pastor beforehand.

774. In the Lord's Supper the unleavened bread and wine are consecrated by the pastor with the words of Christ. Here the Lord Jesus gives into our mouths the same body which carried our sins to the cross and the same blood which washed our sins away. When, with faith, we eat and drink this Holy Communion, we receive the forgiveness of our sins which Christ earned for all people on the cross. Additionally, in this Holy Meal God strengthens our faith. Those who commune without faith or who believe that Christ's body and blood are merely represented, symbolized or spiritually present take the sacrament to their judgment as God says in I Corinthians 11.

The Sacrament of the Altar is a confession of the faith which is confessed at this church. All who commune here are sorry for their sins, trust in the Lord Jesus and in His supper for salvation, believe that the teachings of this church are the true Bible teachings and desire to accept and support the ministry of our church. Any who are not yet instructed, or in doubt of the Sacrament, or who hold to a different confession, or who belong to a different church body, are asked to commune only after they have had a chance to talk to the Pastor.

Invitation to the Communion

775. WELCOME TO THE LORD'S TABLE. In and with the consecrated bread and wine, we here receive the true Body and Blood of our crucified and risen Lord. We trust Christ's promise that this gift is given for all believers for the forgiveness of sins. Communicants who are unable to eat wheat bread or unable to drink wine may receive Holy Communion in just one kind with the assurance that they yet share in all the gifts and graces of this Sacrament. Several prefilled glasses of grape juice are available in each tray of glasses. Those persons not yet communing are encouraged to present themselves at the altar for blessing (please cross your arms over your chest as a signal). All who trust Christ's redeeming presence are here welcomed to gather around His altar like a family around a table, a body around its heart.

776. WELCOME TO THE LORD'S TABLE. All who seek God and are drawn to Christ are welcome at this Communion Table. The ushers will direct you forward to receive the bread and wine. Grape juice is available for those who wish. Those who do not wish to commune are asked to come forward for a blessing. Please cross your arms over our chest as a signal.

777. Communion—At every celebration we share in the Lord's Supper (Holy Communion) Jesus said the broken bread represents My life given for you on the cross, the cup represents My blood shed for you on the cross. We joyfully receive these reminders of God's great gift to us through the death and resurrection of His Son. We invite you to join with us as we take a piece of bread from the broken loaf, dip the bread in the cup (grape juice), and partake.

778. All worshippers are invited to come forward at the time of Communion. Adults and children who are NOT baptized, please cross your arms over your chest and you will receive a prayer of blessing. Baptized children may receive if they and their parents desire it.

779. People of faith are welcome to the Holy Communion. The bread may be received in the hand or mouth, the wine may be received from the traditional chalice or from the tray. The darker glasses in the tray contain alcohol-free grape juice.

780. Communion, also knows as the Lord's Supper, this simple object lesson reminds us that Jesus gave His life for us. We eat a small piece of bread and drink a small cup of grape juice, which represent Jesus' body and blood. If you would like to honor Him with us, we invite you to participate as it is served.

781. IF YOU ARE A GUEST TODAY, please read the statement regarding participation of the Holy Communion in the bulletin.

782. HOLY COMMUNION: We believe in the Doctrine of the Real Presence. Scripture teaches us, according to the promise of our Lord Jesus, that when we receive the Bread and the Wine, we also receive the true Body and Blood of Christ needed for the forgiveness of sins. Accordingly, to receive this promise we must have faith in God's Holy Word regarding this meal. All who believe these promises of Scripture are welcome to commune with us. If you have questions, you may ask the Lay Minister on duty or the Pastor prior to the worship service.

783. If you choose not to participate in the communion do not be embarrassed. Feel free to pass the plate or tray to the person next to you.

784. The Lord's Supper is open to all. Take the bread and cup as it is passed, and partake in unison when invited.

785. A Time of Communion: All are invited to the Table of God for refinement and renewal through the Life of Christ. Communion will be served at two stations. You may receive communion at either station; standing or kneeling at the communion rail. Break off a piece of the bread and dip it into the cup. Stay at the rail as long as you desire. Communion in this church is open to all. We invite you to join in this special meal that celebrates God's mighty actions and special presence in Jesus Christ.

786. We celebrate Holy Communion today and welcome all who believe in Jesus Christ as Lord and Savior to join us. Distribution is continuous. Glasses marked in red are for grape juice. Those who have difficulty in going to the altar should sit in the front pew and communion will be brought to them.

787. Communion—Communion is celebrated once each month, usually on the First of the month. If you have made a personal commitment of faith to follow Jesus Christ, please celebrate with us by taking the bread and cup as they are passed. Hold the bread and cup until you are instructed.

788. THE EUCHARIST—The Lord Jesus invites all the faithful to join together at the Holy Table. All who are baptized and believe in Christ's presence may commune with bread and your choice of either wine or white grape juice (in center of tray). Please follow the directions of the ushers. Those who are first in the pew should ascend the steps and kneel at the rail directly in front of the altar. When the gifts of Christ are given to you, it is appropriate to respond "Amen" or "Thank You" to Him. Stand, join hands and receive the blessing following communion.

789. All baptized Christians instructed in the Sacrament who believe that through the bread and wine we receive Christ's body and blood for the forgiveness of sins are invited to His Table. Non-communing children may come to the altar rail with their families to receive a blessing.

790. Communion—At every celebration we share in the Lord's Supper (Holy Communion). Jesus said the broken bread represents His life given for you on the cross, the cup represents His blood shed for you on the cross. We joyfully receive these reminders of God's great gift to us through the death and resurrection of His Son. We invite you to join with us as we each take a piece of bread from the broken loaf, dip the bread in the cup (grape juice), and partake.

791. Would you like to join us at our Lord's table? Maybe God's Spirit has stirred in you a desire to receive the Lord's Supper. God's Word encourages people wishing to commune to prepare. Maybe the following paragraph will help you in your preparation:

We trust Jesus' Words given to us in the Holy Scriptures. Body and blood are truly present in the bread and wine in a mysterious way. It is a miracle. People who recognize His real presence and are burdened with guilt/remorse over their sins receive His wondrous forgiveness at His table. Those trusting Jesus' Words are invited to commune with their Lord.

If you or your children will not be communing but would desire a spoken blessing, fold your arms as you kneel at the communion railing. The pastor or one of our ministers will speak God's blessing for you.

792. YOU ARE ALL WELCOME, regardless of age or denomination, to share in the consecrated bread and wine at the Lord's Table. Anyone who wishes not to receive the Eucharist, is welcome to receive a blessing at the altar rail. (Indicate this desire by crossing your hands over your chest).

793. The Communion of the People—All are invited to come forward to receive communion or a blessing. Any baptized person who wishes to receive communion is invited to do so. To receive the bread, please place one hand over the other. To receive the cup, please guide the chalice to your lips by gently taking the bottom of the cup in your hands. If you would like to intinct (bread dipped in the wine), a Eucharistic Minister will take the bread from your hand, intinct it and place it in your mouth. If, for any reason, you would prefer not to receive the chalice (the cup of wine), you may cross your arms or touch the chalice, when it is offered to you by a minister who says "The blood of Christ, the cup of salvation."

794. SACRAMENT OF HOLY COMMUNION—We welcome you to this Holy Communion. All are invited to receive.

(8:00) Please put on a name tag and come forward to receive the bread and wine from the stewards and pastor. Receive by intinction (dip bread into cup).

(9:30) The stewards will pass the bread; wine is in the pews.

(11:15) Please put on a name tag and come forward to receive the bread and wine from the stewards and pastor. Receive by intinction (dip bread into cup).

795. Celebration of Holy Communion—Receiving Holy Communion is one of the most important parts of worship. To a child, it says something special happens during the sharing of the Sacrament. Therefore, we encourage all persons, adults and children, to receive communion. Sharing of communion with infants is optional, and is a parent's decision. As you come forward, you may renew your Baptism by dipping into the font and making the sign of the cross upon yourself.

796. You Are Invited—All baptized Christians are welcome to receive Holy Communion at the Altar of this church. Coming forward and receiving the Bread and Wine is to receive Jesus. The invitation to Holy Communion is an Altar Call. Your coming forward and receiving God's gifts is an affirmation or reaffirmation of your faith in Jesus Christ as your personal Lord and Savior. At the Communion station to the right in the front, the Sub-Deacon will minister the Holy Sacrament by intinction, allowing you to partake of the common cup without drinking from it. At the altar step, you will have the option of receiving the Holy Sacrament by intinction or by drinking from the common cup. Please direct your children to receive the Holy Sacrament by intinction.

797. Children are welcome at the altar for a blessing, or with their parents' permission to receive the Sacrament.

798. SPECIAL NOTE TO OUR VISITORS: We are often asked if visitors can receive the Lord's Supper at our church. Since the church feels a Scripturally-founded stewardship responsibility regarding the Lord's Supper, it sets the following guidelines: certainly the communicant must have been baptized. Very much in order also a desire for and acceptance of God's forgiveness, and a thirst for being in unity with one's fellow Christians. We take our Lord's words, "This is My Body," and "This is My Blood" to mean what they say: that the Body and Blood of Christ are actually present in the bread and wine. This is to say that we do not simply memorialize the Last Supper. Rather, we hold that the whole Gospel is embodied in this Sacrament, bringing and assuring us of God's forgiveness and of our fellowship with God and with one another, even as we eat and drink.

799. The Elders will serve you in the pew. It is our custom to eat the bread individually, but hold the cup until everyone has been served so that we may drink together.

800. Invitation to Communion-- All Christians are invited to receive the Sacrament of Holy Communion. The elements will be received by intinction (dipping the bread into the chalice). Both wine and grape juice are available. The white chalice has grape juice. Children are welcome to come with their families to the altar for a special blessing. When you have received communion, please return to your seat as you are ready.

801. All baptized Christians are welcome and encouraged to receive communion, including children of any age. Anyone is welcome to come to the altar rail for a blessing. We hope you will find your worship experience here significant.

802. If you come as a family, you are invited to serve one another.

803. "Come As You Are" Communion, Friday, December 31, 5:00 to 8:00 P.M. Drop in any time. The pastors will serve communion at the altar rail. Materials for silent meditation will be available. Take time out from your work and merry-making to reflect on the past, and look ahead to the new year.

804. Holy Communion is celebrated every Sunday. We welcome you to join us at the altar. If you do not desire communion today, but would like to receive a blessing, you may communicate your desire for a blessing by keeping your hands down when you come forward.

805. Lord's Supper—When receiving the cup, hold it a few moments with Jesus.

806. REGARDING OUR HOLY COMMUNION PRACTICES, we ask that you prepare to receive the Lord's Supper by reading the **Sacramental Registration side of our Welcome-Worship Registration Card.** If communing, please sign both sides of the card and either hand it to an usher when you go up to commune or place it in the collection plate during the Offering. In receiving Christ's true Body and Blood, you may receive the consecrated host either directly to the mouth or first into the palm of your hand. The consecrated wine may be received by common cup (the chalice) or individual chalices. **Those communing with the common cup are ushered first, then those receiving with the individual chalices.**

807. Communion is served to members in their homes if they are ill or unable to come to the regular service.

808. GRAPE JUICE is available in the center of the Communion tray for those who, FOR MEDICAL REASONS are unable to receive the wine.

809. Communion at home or hospital is available on Sunday for those who are ill or shut-in. A lay minister will bring a portion of the consecrated bread and wine we have just shared. Please call the Church office to speak to one of the clergy.

810. As the bread is passed, take, and say to the one passed to "Take and eat with thanksgiving."

811. Lord's Supper—Hold the bread until all are served, symbolizing that we are one body in Christ. Drink the cup as you are served, for we must also have a personal relationship with God through Jesus Christ.

812. The Communion—An elder will pass you the bread. We take it as it comes to us. An elder will pass you the cup. We celebrate and partake of it together. Please bring the cup to the table in the Narthex after the services. The outer ring of each tray contains wine; the inner rings, juice.

813. THE COMMUNION—All is now ready for our Holy Communion with Christ and the members of His Body the Church. As the consecrated elements are distributed to the communicants, we sing a hymn, "Lamb of God" (John 1:29) as a confession of Who it is we are receiving and as a prayer for the blessings of forgiveness, life and salvation which He has promised to give us. Other hymns may also mark our communion devotion. "The Body of Christ given for you; the Blood of Christ shed for you", the ministers say as they give the Sacrament to the people.

814. Post Communion Prayer: "Almighty God, you provide the bread from heaven, your Son, Jesus our Lord. Grant that we who have received the Sacrament of body and blood may abide in Him and He in us. That we may be filled with the power of His endless life now and forever. Amen."

815. An appropriate hymn is sung as the table is cleared.

816. THE COMMUNION DISMISSAL—Now may these gifts that you have received of the Body and Blood of Jesus strengthen you in your faith and empower you to follow Him as Lord. We depart from the Lord's Table in joy and in peace. Amen.

817. CLOSING PRAYER (in unison)—"Loving God, we thank you that you have fed us in this Sacrament, united us with Christ, and given us a foretaste of the heavenly banquet in your eternal kingdom. Send us out in the power of your spirit to live and work to your praise and glory, for the sake of Jesus Christ our Lord. Amen."

818. THE POST COMMUNION—As the Lord's table is cleared, we sing a song of rejoicing. This may be the biblical "Lord, now you let your servant go in peace" (Luke 2:29-32), in which Simeon rejoiced that he had seen Christ, a joy we share because we have received Him in the Sacrament. A final Prayer asks that we may carry out in our lives the implications of Holy Communion. The presiding minister pronounces a Blessing using either a formula similar to the one that began the Service or the Aaronic benediction from the Old Testament (Numbers 6:24-26). A minister speaks word of Dismissal, telling us to "Go in peace; Serve the Lord" in daily life which is also a worship of God. We respond with a shout: "Thanks be to God."

CHAPTER 21

Special Services

In this chapter are listed special service days in chronological order. Some of the ideas were gathered in church services, but others came from books and magazine articles. Christian bookstores have numerous books on this subject.

Special Services

First Sunday of the Year

819. Every member accepts the challenge of bringing at least one unchurched person to church in the coming year.

820. Have Member Dedication Sunday this Sunday.

Valentine Day Sunday

821. Have different members tell how they met their spouses.

April 1 (when it falls on Sunday)

822. Without the song leader's knowledge the congregation had been asked not to sing the first verse.

823. Pastor ready to preach opens his folder to find a note, "We have kidnapped your sermon notes. If you want it back, you will have to sing 'Jesus Loves Me'."

824. Ushers play a practical joke on the pastor by bringing empty offering plates forward.

825. Put in the bulletin the following poem:

The budget here is very sound;
Donations come from all around.
Offerings keep going up
Like an overflowing cup.
Giving extra—that's the rule
There's too much money—
APRIL FOOL.

Sunday before April 15

826. Several weeks before Income Tax date put in the bulletin IRS rules for tax-deductible contributions. The tax law encourages charitable contributions by making them tax-deductible if certain conditions are met. It is important for church members to be familiar with these conditions.

Lent

827. Have a Dramatic Lenten Series Eye Witnesses to a Crucifixion portraying different Biblical characters that witnessed Jesus' crucifixion: Caiaphas, Pilate, Judas, and Peter. Also Mary Magdalene and the crowd calling for the release of Barabbas and the crucifixion of Jesus.

828. On **Palm Sunday** have the congregation meet outside and given palm branches. Then go into the sanctuary representing the entry into Jerusalem, children first, then choir and then worshippers.

829. On **Palm Sunday** give all worshippers small crosses made of strips of bamboo.

830. On **Maundy Thursday** have a worship and fellowship meal with table in the shape of a cross. John 13:34-35

831. On **Maundy Thursday**, **Good Friday** or **Easter Vigil** have the service Tenebrae (gradually extinguishing candles until all is dark).

832. On **Maundy Thursday** announce before hand for quietness and have "QUIET' signs posted. Begin the program by dimming lights, then have Jesus and disciples enter around the table with spotlight on them. They appear to be talking...Jesus serves...Judas leaves, etc.

Good Friday

833. Have members of the church go to one place where someone died from violence, and hold a memorial service. If it is in a home, discuss it with those left behind, and perhaps such a memorial service will open the door to their salvation.

834. Have a candle for each person in the area during the past year who died from violence. Read each name followed by a gong being struck.

835. During the day have an ecumenical service with pastors participating. The offering goes for a non-connected church cause, such as help for the homeless.

836. For the evening service have the lights go out and 12 candles lit at the front of the sanctuary. Then with each disciple's name and his part in the events a candle is snuffed out. In the darkness a soloist, unaccompanied, sings, "Were You There When They Crucified My Lord?" This is followed by someone in the back pounding nails in wood. Then have a recording of thunder and loud ripping of cloth. After a few moments worshippers leave in silence.

Easter

837. Have the names of Easter lilies donors in the worship folder and name in memory of.

838. Have an Easter tree made from three leafless tree branches and decorated by the children with symbol ornaments to remember Christ's resurrection.

839. Have a drama presentation of the resurrection of Lazarus coming forth from the grave bound hand and foot with grave clothes and face bound with a napkin. Jesus says, *"Loose him and let him go."*

840. For the evening service on one side of the sanctuary a misty fog descends; and as it clears, Jesus appears. The account of His appearing to Mary Magdelene and the other Mary—then other appearances—then more fog descends and Jesus disappears.

841. Toward the end of the service ask all worshippers who would like to join the choir in the singing of the beloved *Hallelujah Chorus*, with music available at the front.

Sunday after Easter

842. Call it "Low Sunday" and encourage everyone to come.

843. Call it "Bright Sunday" with humor from pastor and members sharing jokes.

844. Call it "Holy Humor Sunday" with humor from pastor and members.

Mothers Day

845. Give the oldest mother flowers and the newest mother diapers.

846. Recognize the oldest mother and the newest mother, but not the mother with the most children (welfare cases), or the youngest mother (teenage mother-out-of-wedlock).

847. Have carnations given by little girls to all mothers.

848. Have mothers do all the service, including the sermon.

849. Have the kids write “What My Mother Is” and put in bulletin folder insert with the kids’ first names.

850. Sing *She’s Got the Whole World In Her Hands.*

851. Have younger kids sing “Happy Mother’s Day To You” and pass the mike around to hear individual voices.

852. Have different kids recite poems about mother.

Fathers Day

853. Give the oldest father a container for false teeth, or other suitable gift—and the newest father, diapers.

854. Give the oldest father two ties, a narrow tie and a wide tie to be used whenever each is in style, and ask him how many revivals of the wide tie has he has lived through.

855. Have the fathers in charge of the service, including the sermon.

856. Have all fathers wear their wildest tie and have kids judge the winner.

857. Have certain women tell stories of their fathers.

858. Plan a viewing of the film *A Gathering of Men* (Public Affairs Television,267 Broadway, New York, NY 10007 (800-843-0048) during the week before or after Father’s Day.

859. Invite the congregation the week previous to Fathers Day to bring pictures of their fathers to place on and around the altar.

860. Sermon, “Standing In the Gap” Lev. 22:30

Children's Day

861. Have children do all the worship service, even sermon if one is capable, and dedicate to mothers.

862. Give Bibles to all Third graders—an annual occurrence.

863. Give out certificates for perfect Sunday School attendance. Teachers or Sunday School Superintendent calls names, pastor shakes each hand and gives a Bible to each one. Promote this service all year.

864. Everyone sing *I've Got the Joy, Joy, Joy Down In My Heart* and release big beach balls to be bounced around.

865. Have "Operations Andy" (as adults Operation Andrew) and have the kids write down three names to pray for, at least one who doesn't know Jesus.

July Fourth Sunday

866. Call it "Love America Sunday" and have contagious and inspiring music, dance, and narrative, followed by a challenging message from the pastor, then an old-fashioned Dinner On the Grounds.

Halloween

867. Have a church dinner for families with small children; then send them out in costumes to sing Christmas Carols to the homes.

868. Have a program at church with comedians and clowns to counteract the usually ugly and violent observance of Halloween.

All Saints Day

869. In November, recognize loved ones lost within the past year. In bulletin insert have form for family name, deceased loved one, relation, comment about them.

Veterans Day Service

870. Recognize all veterans from each war in the past. Have veterans in charge of the worship service.

Advent

871. Have the Lighting of the Advent Candles, giving the congregation an opportunity to prepare their hearts for Christmas—to reflect on the celebration of the birth of the Lord Jesus Christ.

872. Light a candle on the Advent wreath on each of the four Sundays of Advent. Each candle symbolizes one important part of the Christmas story. The first candle represents the prophecies foretelling the Messiah's birth; the second candle, the town of Bethlehem; the third candle, the shepherds; the fourth candle, the angels. The candles are lit by different members of the church.

Christmas Programs

873. Have shepherds on the stage and the choir in the balcony. Someone reads the account of the shepherds hearing a chorus of heavenly voices while the choir is singing.

874. About half way through the Christmas program have the congregation stand and sing Christmas carols, with words on the screen. As the last carol is being sung have the choir go down and stand around the sanctuary for the next song on the program with the congregation seated.

875. For a Christmas drama have the actors (especially if in costume) line up in the narthex to greet the worshippers as they exit and wish them a Merry Christmas.

876. At the end of the program have the pastor give a humorous announcement about driving home – or have the message on the screen. Examples:

"Drive carefully. Motorists can be recalled by their Maker."

"Drive with care. Life has no spare"

"Please drive carefully—the IRS needs you"

"Driving is a lot like baseball—It's the number of times you get home safely that counts."

877. If the Christmas program calls for a solo, duet, or trio, have their names on the screen.

878. Have an expensive looking program folder with "Printing donated by___________" (individual, family, organization, or business).

879. Have a Living Christmas Tree Musical with choir members in blending robes standing in the form of a huge Christmas tree. Have substitutes for any vacancies on the tree. Have a recent convert's testimony. Each choir member has a flashlight or spotlight highlighting the form of a Christmas tree and at the end the lights are transformed to a cross while the singers sing the Hallelujah Chorus. Have a short message on the meaning of the cross.

880. Each worshipper has a candle which is lit by the candle of a neighbor starting with the aisle. Message, Matthew 5:14-16

881. Have kids write a Christmas play and be the characters in it.

Christmas Sunday

882. Have a "Come Home For Christmas" campaign in December to encourage attendance of inactive members.

883. Have members visit other churches to get ideas for Christmas programs.

New Years Eve
(or Sunday Before New Years Day)

884. Have forms for evaluation—(1) What I like about my church, (2) What I would like to see changed; mail it to all members with a self-addressed stamped envelope to return after getting approval from the Church Board.

Church Anniversary Sunday

885. For twelve months before Anniversary Sunday, one Sunday a month, have a charter member give a brief memory moment.

886. Have an Anniversary Motto, such as: "Looking in the Year-view Mirror" or "Life Begins at 40 (or 50)."

887. Have Anniversary T-shirts.

888. Have an Anniversary Anthology which includes the history of the church, letters from denominational leaders, former pastors, etc. Have a message from the current pastor. Have pictures of past pastors, and pictures of the church and members in the past.

889. Have members and former members bring a note of appreciation to be hung on the line in the foyer.

890. Have charter members participate in the service; Scripture reading, prayer, ushers, special music, etc.

891. Have a local photo studio take family pictures—sign-up sheets for date, time, family, phone number. See if the photographer will take the first photo free and charge for extras.

892. Put in the worship folder: "This occasion gives us the opportunity to shake hands with old faces."

893. "Everyone cup your hands in front of you—the future of this church is in your hands."

894. Before Anniversary Day ask members to help in the welcoming of guests on Anniversary Sunday. An hour or two of work to spread the jobs evenly tasks include

(1) Sunday morning set-up;
(2) Cookies and punch serving;
(3) Servers at the banquet;
(4) "No-host" bar servers;
(5) Ticket-Memorabilia sales; Balloons;
(6) Yard monitor for children;
(7) Clean-up afterwards.

895. Have a Wedding Fashion Show before the Anniversary. Ask for all types of wedding clothing (traditional, non-traditional, bridal gowns, groom's attire, attendant clothes, children's clothing, etc.)

896. Read letters from those who could not come.

897. Have past pastors take part in the service.

898. At the beginning of the service recognize any charter members present and name those who could not come.

899. Thirty minutes before the service meet in the social hall for socializing. Then after service have a pot-luck dinner.

900. All choir members in the past _______years come to the front and sing a familiar song, as *Oh God, Our Help in Ages Past.*

901. Introduce each past pastor, and have those in the congregation to stand if they were there during his/her pastorate—baptized, married, joined church, became Christians, babies dedicated, etc.

Pastor's Anniversary Sunday

902. Have a large sign "WELCOME TO PASTOR AND WIFE'S________ ANNIVERSARY."

903. Have a sign " O MAN WORTHY OF DOUBLE HONOR" I Tim. 5:19

904. When honoring the pastor have a bouquet of roses for the First Lady.

905. Have limited time for testimonials by different members.

906. When pastor retires or leaves the church, have the youth come forward and lay hands on pastor and each pray.

No Excuses Sunday

907. The Sunday before, have in the foyer items parishioners can take for **No Excuses Sunday:**

a. Blankets and sweaters for those who don't come because the church is too cold.
b. Fans for those who stay away because the church is too hot.
c. Hard hats for those afraid the roof will fall in;
d. Stop watches and whistles for those who think the sermon is too long.
e. Cushions for those who think the pews are too hard;
f. Name tags for those who are afraid they won't be noticed.

Bring a Friend Sunday

908. Promote for months. Have buttons as walking billboards; Radio announcements and newspapers, fliers, banners at the church.

909. Have an "Invite a Friend Sunday" once or twice a year with the Gospel presented in an non-threatening way—no altar calls. After the service have a Coffee and Conversation Hour in honor of our friends. Follow-up letter from the pastor.

Bible Sunday

910. Have families pledge to read the Bible daily. Have all children Grades 3-6 with their parents and with their Bibles with one verse highlighted. Each family reads that verse—either parent, child, or all together.

Week of Fasting

911. Pastor asks all those who will fast on Monday raise hands... Tuesday...Wednesday...Thursday...Friday...Saturday... Sunday...

Dedication Sunday

912. Call it "Time for the Sermon on the Amount."

Evangelistic Month

913. Have a **FRAN**tastic Month, reaching **F**riends, **R**elatives, **A**ssociates, and **N**eighbors. First Sunday is FRIENDS DAY; second Sunday is RELATIVES DAY; third Sunday is ASSOCIATES DAY; fourth Sunday is NEIGHBORS DAY.

914. Have a "Celebration Sunday" for members to invite unchurched friends and relatives to the worship service.

Kids and Family Worship Sunday

915. Have regular service with selected members giving short message on regular church attendance, then pastor gives message

Senior Outreach Sunday

916. Have special prayer during the worship service for those in retirement and convalescence homes. Visit and/or write letters and cards.

International Sunday

917. Recognize foreign-born members and members married to foreign-born; then have members bringing dishes from their countries.

CHAPTER 22

Outreach

This Chapter lists different groups and how they can do an effective outreach service.

Church members need to realize that their responsibility is to BE the church, not just to ATTEND the services. It used to be that the pastor was the minister of the church; but today most churches emphasize that the members are the ministers.

Outreach

918. Have a CLASS ministry (**C**hrist's **L**ove **A**longside **S**omeone **S**uffering) for all who have a loved one who is an alcoholic, an addict, or any compulsion that holds them in bondage.

919. Have an ADAM ministry (**A**lcohol, **D**rug **A**buse **M**inistry) with leaders who have been "Where you are today." Through group discussion based on Alcoholics Anonymous, giving hope to the chemically dependent and strength to the leaders.

920. Have a BRIDGE ministry (**B**eginning **R**ecovery in **D**espair and **G**rief **E**xperience).

921. Have a CARE ministry (**C**ontact **A**nd **R**each **E**veryone).

922. Have a DAWN ministry (**D**iscipling **A** **W**hole **N**ation).

923. Have a SEND ministry (**S**tart, **E**vangelize, **N**urture, **D**evelop).

924. In the bulletin, "Our church is a 7-day Christ-centered Evangelistic Community"; and then list the names of those who evangelized, who visited hospita patients, who sent cards or visited shut-ins, who baby-sat for someone in church, who helped members move, etc.

925. Have a coupon in the Yellow Pages for a "FREE TRIP TO HEAVEN," (appendix Bulletin Board Sayings #48 or #72).

926. Have your church go to a local baseball game with tail-gate party, and invite guests.

927. In your parking lot advertise free breakfasts Sunday mornings and have Sunday School on the lot.

928. Have a Church Neighborhood Watch program with reference to the program by the police department.

929. Have opportunity for members and friends to donate blood. List dates, time, place for donations.

930. Have a community counseling center staffed by Christian professionals to provide a safe and confidential relationship to enable people to become whole persons emotionally, relationally, and spiritually. In order to provide quality service and facilities, charge a fee for all counseling, therapy, testing, groups and classes.

931. Sponsor a community blood drive.

932. In the yellow pages list a number to call for a three-minute sermon.

933. Have a City Work Day once or twice a year. Members tackle needed jobs in the city. Church furnishes lunch. (City is more apt to rule in favor of church requests in the future).

934. In metropolitan areas advertise in yellow pages with cross street as well as street number.

935. Start a Creative Writers Group.

936. If near a farm or field—as sweet corn or fruit—where crops are not picked due to shortage of labor or produce remaining after harvest, have a Gleaning Group (God's Gleaning Group) to pick for the needy. If this is a news item for the news media, it is good publicity for the church.

937. Have a Car Ministry—members and others donate cars in need of repair. Members who are mechanics repair them and teach would-be-mechanics. Cars are then given to the needy, such as single mothers, workers who have been laid off, etc.

938. Have a Bear Ministry—Give teddy bears to people of all ages who need a friend. Work with local hospital, YMCA and YWCA and other community service organizations.

939. In the September bulletin, "Christmas comes soon for our missionaries. We will be taking donations in October, as they need to be sent by the end of October or beginning of November."

CHAPTER 23

Coping Situations

What do you do if during a worship service someone's cell phone rings? This could be an embarrassing position for every one, or it could be turned into a humorous situaton if the pastor says something like, "If that is God calling, tell him you are doubling your giving."

Another coping situation is when the lights go out. The pastor could say, "Will someone please call the electric company and tell them that the check is in the mail?"

Or during a heavy downpour the pastor could say, "Isn't that just like God? Here we are inside praising His name, and He is outside washing our cars!"

This chapter addresses other interruptions and how they can be handled in a humorous way—kids misbehaving, noises outside/inside, uninvited guests such as a fly or bee flying around in the sanctuary, a baby crying, odors, air conditioning not working, etc. There are seven ideas for coping with low attendance and what to say to a drowsy congregation. The final idea, #1001, deals with worshippers sitting in back.

It is helpful if the pastor is prepared for unexpected situations to have something to say on the lighter side to allay any concern on the part of the worshipper-- for example, if the lights go out, the pastor says, "Will someone please call the electric company and tell them the check is in the mail?"

The 62 ideas in this chapter have been subdivided to help reduce the total number to 1001.

Coping Situations

Weather

940. Thank God for bad weather. It gives us a chance to show our loyalty to God and to the church. God bless you who have come out on a day like this.

941. Some of our members may have stayed home because of the rain. Personally we here like inclement weather so we can show the Lord that a little rain won't keep us from church.

942. The Lord will come in a cloud, and it won't make any difference whether it is raining or not.

943. Don't knock the weather. If it didn't change once in a while, nine out of ten people couldn't start a conversation.

944. (Heavy downpour) If you think this is bad, what about the people and animals on Noah's Ark? Can you imagine it raining like this for forty days and forty nights? And they had never experienced rain. After a month of heavy downpour with no end in sight think what it was like in the Ark. Here inside the church during this downpour, it is relatively quiet. Consider the situation in the Ark, with all the braying and barking and howling and yelping. Today, we hear the noise of rain on the roof, but I suppose the noise of the animals in the Ark drowned out the noise of the rain. Aren't we the lucky ones?

945. (Burst of thunder) This reminds me of the three-year-old girl who became really frightened by a burst of thunder. She ran to her parents' bedroom, "Mommy, I'm scared." The mother said, "Go back to your room. God will be there with you." The little girl thought for a while, and then said, "Mommy, I'll sleep with Daddy, and you can go to my room and sleep with God."

946. (Air conditioning on too high) You've got the air conditioner on Siberia again.

947. (No air conditioning) You young people want to know what it was like in the good old days? Well, now you know.

948. (Hot weather) It is hot in here, and the air conditioning is not working. Because of this you may choose which of the three sermons I have prepared. I have thousand dollar sermon which lasts fifteen minutes, a five hundred dollar sermon which lasts thirty minutes, and a one hundred dollar sermon which lasts for one hour. The ushers will now pass the collection plates to see which sermon you want.

949. (Hot weather) This hot weather reminds me of the housewife who had invited a number of guests to her home for dinner; and when they were all seated around the table, she was in the kitchen and said to her six-year-old son, "I think it would be nice if you said the blessing."

The little boy thought for a moment and then said, "I don't know what to say."

His mother answered, "Oh, yes, you do. Just say what you've heard me say. It begins, 'O Lord...'"

So the little boy, bowing his head, said, "Oh Lord, why in the world did I invite these people here on a boiling hot day like this?"

I just hope you have a good reason for coming to church today.

950. (Hot weather) If you think it is hot here, hell is hotter; don't go there.

Noises

951. (Loud noise, as Jet sonic boom) One of these days we are going to hear a much louder noise than which we have just heard. The trumpet will sound, and the heaven shall pass away with a great noise. 2 Peter 3:10

952. (Loud noise) I haven't heard that much noise since I witnessed a collision between a truck load of empty milk cans and a truck of geese.

953. (Coughing) Ushers have cough drops ready.

954. (Baby crying) Did I say something that upset that little tyke?

955. (Baby crying) Crying babies during a church service is like New Year's resolutions: they need to be carried out.

956. (Coughing during service) Say, "Give the lady (gentleman) a glass of water." Then tell a story while usher is getting the water. Say, "Now, what was I saying: Oh, yes, 'Give the lady a glass of water'."

957. (Fire engine passing by) Apparently there is a fire someplace and a fire engine has been dispatched to put out the fire. But there is a place of everlasting fire where all the engines in the world could not begin to put out. The story is told of the Texan who died and went to heaven. As St. Peter was showing him around heaven and pointing out the heavenly features, the Texan would brag that there were bigger and better features in Texas.

Finally St. Peter became so agitated that he took the Texan to the edge of heaven where he could look down on hell. "I bet you don't have anything like that in Texas."

"No, but I know some ole boys down in Houston who could put it out."

Now we can laugh at that story, but hell is no laughing matter. Perhaps this would be a good time to preach on eternal punishment, but all I want to say now is that whether or not you believe in a literal hell of fire and brimstone, you can not dispute the fact that you will be separated from God throughout all eternity if you have not made preparations, or reservations.

958. (Laughter) Now there's a happy one.

959. (Laughter) She didn't mean to. She was smiling and the smile busted.

960. (Kid whistling during pastor's prayer; after prayer) I suppose you asked God to teach you how to whistle and just then He did.

961. (Snoring) Thank God he has the ability to relax.

962. (Snoring) This reminds me of the man who invariably went to sleep during the sermon. Finally he died and left the church $50,000 because he had been troubled with insomnia and the only time and place he could sleep was in church.

963. (Snoring) A man asked his doctor if there was anything he could do for his snoring. The doctor asked if the man's snoring disturbed his wife.

"Yes, and the rest of the congregation as well."

964. (Sneezing) The origin of "God bless you" is nothing to sneeze at. An old superstition had it that when someone sneezed, the soul momentarily left the body. This enabled the devil to creep in and prevent the return of the soul. But by saying "God bless you" the devil was stopped from entering the body.

Uninvited Guests

965. (A bird, fly, or bee flying around in sanctuary) In seminary we were taught homiletics but not how to deal with unwelcomed guests.

966. (Same situation) Let's take the optimistic approach to this situation. This bird (fly, bee) is just trying to find a way out.

967. (A Bird) Is this a bird of paradise?

968. (A Bird) We will now take up bird-watching.

969. (A Bird) We have a problem, but that bird has a bigger problem.

970. (A Bird) If that bird could be caught, it would be a bird in the hand is worth two in the bush.

971. (A Fly) Why don't you go back to the kitchen where you belong?

972. (A Fly) If this fly were in my house, I could tell if it was a male or female fly. How? If it landed on a mirror, it would be a female. If it landed on food, it would be a male fly.

973. (A Bee) Bees fly thousands of miles to gather enough nectar to make a pound of honey. Then someone comes along and steals it from them. Perhaps this is why bees have such a lousy disposition.

974. (A Bee) Think about this for a minute. Bees can make you uneasy without ever stinging you. The same thing could be said about our consciences. They also can make us feel uneasy, without ever stinging us.

975. (A Fly or Bee) Is. 7:18 says, *"And it shall come to pass on that day that the Lord shall whistle for the fly that is in the uttermost part of the rivers of Egypt, and for the bee that is in the land of Assyria."*

Kids Misbehaving

976. If you boys don't settle down, I will lose my place and have to start all over again.

977. (Kid running down aisle) Pastor makes reference to Jerry Rice or other football receiver.

978. (Kid running down aisle) The next time your mother goes to the grocery store have her ask the manager if there is some cereal that will sap a kid's energy.

979. (Parent taking out misbehaving child) I heard of one kid being taken out of the service for misbehaving, and as they were at the back of the sanctuary the kid turned around and said, "Pray for me."

980. (Noisy persons) There was a preacher who was an expert in human relations. He did not scold or manifest any sign of anger. He said that he was always reluctant to expose those who misbehave during services because of an experience he had some years ago. A young man who sat in front of him was laughing and making grimaces. He was annoyed and rebuked him severely. Later he was told that he had made a grave mistake. The man he had reproved was an idiot.

Low Attendance

981. Never apologize. Jesus did not say *"Where two or three hundred are gathered in my name..."*

982. Many saints are not here. I just hope the Rapture has not taken place.

983. There are not many here this morning. Let us sing as though there were a thousand.

984. I notice that there are not too many people here this evening. It puts me in mind of the small boy who said to his father: 'I'm supposed to tell you that there's going to be a small PTA meeting tomorrow night.' His father said, "Well, if it is going to be a small one, do I have to go?"

The boy answered, "'Oh, Yes. It's just you and me and the principal."

985. If absence makes the heart grow fonder, a lot of folks must love our church.

986. I realize that fewer people turned out this evening than expected. I remember a story that Abraham Lincoln often told on himself. He made a speech to a very small audience while a blizzard was raging outside. When he finished there was hardly any applause, and there actually were some hisses and boos. After the audience had filed out, the janitor was helping Mr. Lincoln on with his coat and noticed how depressed he was and said, "Mr. Lincoln, don't pay any attention to the way the audience treated you. They don't have any sense. Anybody with any sense stayed home tonight."

987. I notice that the room is not filled to overflowing. Some of you might even have wondered whether I would be willing to preach to a small audience; but let me reassure you on that point by telling you about the preacher who, when he arrived at the church found that only one person present. He waited for others to arrive, but no one else came. So he went to the one-man audience and said to him, "Do you think I should preach my sermon to only one person?"

The man answered, "Well, I am from Montana and all I know is cattle. And I know that if I took a load of feed down to the cattle and only one steer showed up, I certainly would feed him."

Accordingly, the preacher got behind the pulpit and started preaching. Despise the size of his congregation, as he preached he began to get warmed up; and soon he was raising his voice, pounding the pulpit, shaking his fist, and emphasizing every sentence with wild gestures as if he were talking to a thousand people. An hour later when he finished, he came off the platform and said to his one-man audience, "Well, what did you think of my sermon?"

The man answered, "You know, I'm from Montana, and all I know is cattle; but if I took a load of feed down to the cattle and only one steer showed up, I sure wouldn't give him the whole load."

Other Situations

988. (Member of congregation from time to time adds his comments to the sermon) Pastor says, "That's right, Brother" and keeps on with the sermon.

989. (Pastor, reading a note handed to him) This is not a call to worship, but a call to turn off the lights of a 1999 Taurus...when we stand to greet one another.

990. (Pastor, reading a note) The lights of a Lincoln Continental (or other large car) were left on, and the Volkswagon in front of it is beginning to melt."

991. (Pastor, reading a note) The owner of car license number __________was so anxious to get to church they left their lights on.

992. (Pastor or Scripture reader stumbles over Scripture reading) I must have gotten my eye off the Word of God.

993. (The pastor is ill or otherwise not available) Write the sermon and have different lay persons read portions of sermon.

994. (Odor of gas smell) If severe, have ushers call fire department and keep congregation calm with orderly evacuation. Otherwise, tell the story of the mother skunk teaching her offspring how to cope with danger:

"We turn our backs and I will say 'LET US SPRAY.'"

995. (Odor from unknown origin) A cowboy went to church for the first time in his life. When he got back to the ranch, someone asked him how it went.

"I rode up on my horse and tied it in the corral."

His friend said, "You don't mean corral, you mean parking lot."

"I don't know, maybe that 's what they call it. Anyhow, I then went through the main gate."

"You don't mean the main gate, you mean the front door of the church."

"Anyway, a couple of guys took me down the long chute."

"You don't mean long chute, you mean the center aisle."

"Whatever, then they put me in one of those box stalls."

"You don't mean a stall, you mean a pew'."

The cowboy then said, "O, yes, now I remember, that's what the lady said when I sat down beside her. "

996. (Drowsy congregation) It is said that John Wesley was speaking to a drowsy congregation, when he suddenly yelled "FIRE, FIRE!"'

One startled listener woke up and said "WHERE?"

Wesley replied, "In hell for those who sleep during the sermon."

997. (Drowsy congregation, preacher interrupts sermon) The best years of my life were spent in the arms of another man's wife...That was my mother.

998. (Drowsy congregation) Now, you people pay attention—Don't let your ears just hang there doing nothing.

999. (Gloomy audience) Why so glum? You people are looking at me like I was your daughter's first date.

1000. (Speaker realizing he has talked too long) You know, I don't mind your looking at your watches to see what time it is; but it really annoys me when you put them up to your ears to see if they are still running.

1001. (Worshippers sitting in back) I'm going to sit down and give you saints in the back time to move to the front. When you have moved, I'll speak.

Bulletin Board Sayings
General Slogans
Identity Slogans
Mission Slogans
Invitational Slogans

Bulletin Board Sayings

1. "A Bible In The Hand Is Worth Two In The Bookcase."
2. "A Bible That Is Falling Apart Often Belongs To One Who Isn't."
3. "A Christian Has Not Lost The Power To Sin, But The Desire To Sin."
4. "A Christian Is A Living Sermon, Whether Or Not He Preaches A Word."
5. "A Christian Is One Who Makes It Easier For Others To Believe In God."
6. "A Christian Must Get On His Knees Before He Can Get On His Feet."
7. "A Friend Is Someone Who Is There When Good Times Aren't."
8. "A Grounded Christian Life Is Electrifying."
9. "A Lot Of Kneeling Keeps You In Good Standing With God."
10. "A Man Without Religion Is Like A Car Without A Steering Wheel."
11. "A Man Without Religion Is Like A Horse Without A Bridle."
12. "An Empty Tomb Proves Christianity—An Empty Church Denies It."
13. "Anger Is Just One Letter Short Of Danger."
14. "Anyone Who Angers You Conquers You."
15. "Author Of The World's Best-Selling Book—Here This Sunday."
16. "Bank On It—God's Interest In You Never Changes."
17. "Before Passing Judgment On A Sermon, Be Sure To Try It Out In Practice."
18. "Beware Of The Christian With An Open Mouth But A Closed Pocketbook."
19. "Bible Verses Will Save You From Spiritual Reverses."
20. "Carrying A Bible Will Never Take The Place Of Reading It."
21. "Christ Was A Child Who Knew More Than His Parents, Yet He Obeyed Them."
22. "Christians Are The Light Of The World, But The Switch Must Be Turned On."
23. "Christians May Not See Eye-To-Eye, But They Can Walk Arm-In-Arm."
24. "Christmas: It's A Boy!"
25. "Church Is A Place Where You Can Meet Old Friends You Never Saw Before."
26. "Church Membership Is Not Necessarily An Elevator To Heaven."
27. "Cleanliness May Be Next To Godliness, But It Is Not A Substitute."
28. "Come On In And Tithe One On During The Offering."
29. "Come To Church Sunday. If You Have No Sins, Bring Someone Who Has."
30. "Confess Your Own Sins, Not Your Neighbor's."
31. "Confessing Your Sins Is No Substitute For Forsaking Them."
32. "Confessions Heard Every Monday From Weekend Fishermen."
33. "Do Something! Either Lead, Follow, Or Get Out Of The Way."
34. "Do Unto Others As Though You Were The Others."
35. "Do You Know The 23rd Psalm Better Than The Shepherd?"

36. “Don’t Be A Carbon Copy Of Something, Make Our Own Impression.”
37. “Don’t Criticize The Bible—Let The Bible Criticize You.”
38. “Don’t Give The Impression You Have Been Baptized In Vinegar.”
39. “Don’t Wait For The Hearse To Bring You To Church.”
40. “Drive Carefully—Motorists Can Be Recalled By Their Maker.”
41. “Each Day Is A Gift From God: That’s Why It Is Called The Present.”
42. “Faith Builds A Bridge From This World To The Next.”
43. “Faith Without Works Is Like An Automobile Without Gas.”
44. “Fear Not Tomorrow—God Is Already There.”
45. “Feed Your Faith, And Doubts Will Starve To Death.”
46. “Fellowship? We’re All In This Boat Together.”
47. “Fire Insurance Sold Here—Rather Bought.”
48. “Free Trip To Heaven—Details Inside.”
49. “Getting Old? Jesus Can Put A New Wrinkle In Your Life.”
50. “Go To Church For A Beauty Treatment—Get Your Faith Lifted.”
51. “God Does Not Call Us To Be Successful—He Calls Us To Be Faithful.”
52. “God Is Never More Than A Prayer Away.”
53. “God Never Tires Of Hearing Us In Prayer.”
54. “God Promises A Safe Landing, But Not A Calm Voyage.”
55. “God Shocked The World With A Babe, Not A Bomb.”
56. “God Still Speaks To Those Who Take Time To Listen.”
57. “Happy Hour Now In Progress.”
58. “Have Character—Don’t Be One.”
59. “Have You Hugged Your Pastor Today?”
60. “Heaven Knows When You Were Here Last.”
61. “If God Is Small Enough For Us To Understand, He Isn’t Big Enough For Us To Worship.”
62. “If God Seems Far Away, Who Made The First Move?”
63. “If Life Is In Darkness, Turn On The Light.”
64. “If People Have To Ask You If You Are A Christian, Perhaps You’re Not.”
65. “If The Wages Of Sin Is Death, Shouldn’t You Quit Before Payday?”
66. “If You Are Headed In The Wrong Direction, God Allows U-Turns.”
67. “If You Are Too Busy To Pray, You Are Too Busy.”
68. “If You Couldn’t Get Another Bible, What Would Yours Be Worth?”
69. “If You Don’t Like The Way You Were Born, Try Being Born Again.”
70. “If You Think You’re Too Cool For God, You’ll Warm Up.”
71. “If Your Religion Leaves Your Life Unchanged, You’d Better Change Religions.
72. “Interested In Going To Heaven? Apply Here For Flight Training.”
73. “It Was Bitter Experience That Put The Prod Into The Prodigal Son.”
74. “It Is A Terrible Responsibility To Own A Bible.”
75. “It Is Generally In The Summer That Religion Is Snowed Under.”
76. “It’s Nice To Be Important, But It’s More Important To Be Nice.”
77. “It’s Not Where You’ve Been That Matters—But Where You Are Going.”

78. "Join Our Sit-In Demonstration Every Sunday."
79. "Keep Your Bible Open, And You Will Not Find The Door To Heaven Shut."
80. "Leave For Church Early Enough So You Won't Get A Ticket For Speeding."
81. "Leave For Church Early To Get A Back Seat."
82. "Life Is Fragile—Handle With Prayer."
83. "Life's Heaviest Burden Is To Have Nothing To Carry."
84. "Living Without Faith Is Like Driving In A Fog."
85. "Never Be Afraid To Trust An Unknown Future To A Known God."
86. "Never Put A Question Mark Where God Has Put A Period."
87. "No God...No Peace; Know God...Know Peace."
88. "Old Preachers Never Die; Just Turn Them Out To Pastor."
89. "On Pins And Needles? Jesus Will Cushion You."
90. "Our Favorite Attitude Should Be Gratitude."
91. "Our P.A. System Guarantees A Sound Sermon."
92. "Our Sundays Are Better Than Baskin-Robbins."
93. "Patience Is A Virtue That Carries A Lot Of Wait."
94. "Read Your Bible—A Chapter A Day Keeps The Devil Away."
95. "Religion At Its Best Is A Lift, And Not A Load."
96. "Religion Costs, But Irreligion Costs More."
97. "Religion Doesn't Fail People—It's The People Who Fail Religion."
98. "Religion Is Bread For Daily Use, Not Cake For Special Occasions."
99. "Religion Is Life; Faith Is The Only Fuse."
100. "Satan Is Not Afraid Of A Bible With Dust On It."
101. "Searching For A New Look? Have Your Faith Lifted Here."
102. "Since You Can't Take It With You, Why Not Leave It Here?"
103. "Some People Pray For A Bushel But Carry A Spoon."
104. "Sorry, But The Fruit Of The Spirit Doesn't Include Sour Grapes."
105. "Soul Food Served At Every Service."
106. "Spiritual Health And Fitness Club."
107. "Study The Bible To Be Wise; Believe It To Be Safe; Practice It To Be Holy."
108. "Sunday's Special—In By 11, Out By 12"
109. "Thanksgiving: No Whining, Only Dining."
110. "The Bible Contains The Vitamins For A Healthy Soul."
111. "The Bible Is Most Helpful When It Is Open."
112. "The Bible Promises No Loaves To The Loafer."
113. "The Church Needs Workers, Not A Wrecking Crew."
114. "The Competition Is Terrible, But We Are Still In Business."
115. "The Difficulties Of Life Are Intended To Make Us Better, Not Bitter."
116. "The Easiest Thing To Find Is Fault."
117. "The Family Altar Would Altar Many A Family."
118. "The Great Physician Still Makes House Calls"
119. "The Heart Of God Is Never In Need Of A Bypass."
120. "The Lord Gives Us Our Faces—But We Must Provide The Expression."

121. "The Lord Loveth A Cheerful Giver; He Also Accepteth From A Grouch."
122. "The Pits Of Life Can Sprout A Peach Of A Person."
123. "The Poor Man Who Walks With God Is Happier Than The Rich Man Who Rides In A Limousine Without Him."
124. "The Soul Without Prayer Is Like Lungs Without Air."
125. "The Study Of Truth Keeps An Open Dictionary, An Open Mind, And An Open Bible"
126. "The Surest Steps To Heaven Are The Church Steps."
127. "The Sword Of The Spirit Never Becomes Dull From Use."
128. "The World At Its Worst Needs The Church At Its Best."
129. "There Is Plenty Of Heavenly Music For Those Who Are Tuned In."
130. "This Church Is Prayer Conditioned."
131. "Those Who Don't Read The Bible Have No Advantage Over Those Who Can't Read It."
132. "To The Truly Religious Person, Every Day Is Sunday."
133. "Trashed? God Can Recycle You."
134. "Wanted; Large Mouth Bass For Church Choir."
135. "We Are Not Looking For The Undertaker; We Are Looking For The Uppertaker."
136. "We Have A Prophet-Sharing Plan For You."
137. "We Should Study The Bible As A Privilege, Not As A Duty."
138. "We Welcome All Denominations--$1, $5, $10, $20, $50, $100."
139. "What The World Needs Is An Amplifier For The Still, Small Voice."
140. "When The Outlook Is Bad, Try The Uplook."
141. "When There Seems No Way Out, Let God In."
142. "When We Let God Guide, He Will Provide."
143. "When You Get To The End Of Your Rope, Be Thankful—God Is There."
144. "Where There Is No Thirst For Righteousness The Sermon Is Always Dry."
145. "Why Not Let God Have Your Life? He Can Do More With It Than You Can."
146. "Work For The Lord. The Pay Isn't Much, But The Retirement Plan Is Out Of This World."
147. "You Can Buy Education, But Wisdom Is From God."
148. "You Can Not Carry A Cross And A Prejudice At The Same Time."
149. "You Can Not Live In Doubt When You Pray In Faith."
150. "You Can Not Stumble If You Are On Your Knees."
151. "You Don't Get Dizzy Spells From Doing Good Turns."
152. "Your Favorite Attitude Should Be Gratitude."
153. "Your Willful Absence From Church Is A Vote To Close Its Doors."
154. "Zacchaeus Went Out On A Limb For Jesus."

Slogans: General

1. A Changeless Message For A Changing World
2. A Life-changing Experience
3. A New Walk In The Old Path
4. A Place of Healing; A Place of Refreshing
5. A Vision For The People...A People For The Vision
6. A Worshipping Family Of The King
7. All the Gospel for All the People
8. Always A Message Of Hope
9. Because God So Loved The World
10. CAUTION: Lives Under Construction
11. Christ and Family Together
12. Christ Preeminent In All Things
13. Christ's Love In Action
14. Church-centered...Bible-based
15. Different To Make A Difference
16. Enter To Worship...Depart To Serve
17. Exciting Christianity
18. Expository Preaching And Praise
19. Faith Comes By Hearing And Hearing By The Word Of God
20. Family Friendly
21. Famous For The Gospel
22. God In Us For Others...God In Others For Us
23. God Our Father...Christ Our Redeemer...Christ Our Brother
24. God's Riches At Christ's Expense
25. He Cares...We Care
26. In The Heart Of The City, For The Hearts Of The People
27. In The Heart Of The Community With The Community On Its Heart
28. In Touch With Tradition...In Step With The Times
29. It's Not Where We've Been That Matters; But Where We Are Going
30. Jesus Christ, The Same Yesterday, Today and Forever
31. Joyful in Song, Earnest In The Holy Spirit, Satisfying The Soul, Uplifting His Name
32. L.I.F.E.—Love, Inspiration, Friendship, Encouragement
33. Love, Inspiration, Friendship, Encouragement
34. Love, Peace, and Togetherness
35. Loving God in Front of People; Loving People in Front of God
36. Music And Worship That Lifts the Spirit
37. New Testament Christianity Today
38. No Religion, Just Jesus
39. Not For The Faint Of Heart
40. Not Just Friendly...But Friends

41. Our Vision To Your Future
42. Our Worldwide Outreach Ministry Reaches Out To Foreign Countries
43. People Loving People
44. Practical Help for Daily Living From the Word of God
45. Rooted In The Word...Reaching For The World
46. Salvation For The Lost And Strength For The Saints
47. Smaller In Number, Bigger In Heart
48. Success Begins On Sunday
49. Thank God It's Sunday
50. The Bible Sincerely Believed And Faithfully Taught
51. The Bible...Our Rules of Faith and Practice
52. The Difference Is Worth The Distance
53. The Living God And His Word Make The Difference
54. The Love of God Has Made Us a Family
55. The Pain Stops Here
56. The Unchanging Word For a Changing World
57. The Word of God Will Stand Forever (Isaiah 40:8)
58. Theme For (Year): "God Is So Good"
59. There Is No Ship Like Fellowship
60. To God Be The Glory
61. To Know God And To Make Him Known
62. Truth For Today's World
63. United, Equipped, and Empowered To Serve (Eph. 4:11-16)
64. Vibrantly Alive for Christ and the World
65. We Can Do All things Through Christ Who Strengthens Us
66. We Care
67. We Dare To Be Different
68. We Have No Creed But Christ
69. We Love To Sing And Praise The Lord
70. We Share Because We Care
71. What God Has Promised He Is Able To Perform
72. Where The Son Always Shines
73. Whole Gospel To The Whole World
74. Worship, Training, Mission

Slogan Identity

1. A Beacon of Hope To Our Neighborhood
2. A Beautiful Church For Beautiful People
3. A Bible Center Dedicated to Ministering the Uncompromised Word of Faith to the Entire Family
4. A Bible Centered Assembly Where Love Rules
5. A Bible-Believing, Bible-Teaching, World-Reaching Ministry
6. A Bible Teaching Family Church
7. A Bible Teaching Church that Is Looking to Serve People
8. A Bridge to the Peace of Life
9. A Caring and Sharing Intergenerational Family
10. A Caring Church
11. A Caring Church in a Broken World
12. A Caring Church in a Hurting Community
13. A Caring Church For a Changing Community
14. A Caring Community For All Ages
15. A Church All Can Call Home
16. A Church and a Pastor With a Vision
17. A Church Centered on Christ and Community
18. A Church Committed to Christ Through Worship, Nurture, Care, and Growth
19. A Church Dedicated to the Presence of God
20. A Church Designed with Spiritual Growth in Mind
21. A Church Desperate for the Presence of God
22. A Church Filled With The Spirit & All Kinds of People
23. A Church Focused on the Family
24. A Church for All Ages
25. A Church for All Occasions
26. A Church for All People
27. A Church for Every Person and Every Need
28. A Church for Families and Those Who Need One
29. A Church for Our Times
30. A Church for Seekers of Jesus
31. A Church For the Overcomer
32. A Church For Those Who Know Where They're Going, Also For Those Who Don't
33. A Church for Today's People Where the Bible Is Taught In Balance and Truth
34. A Church Large Enough to Serve You, and Small Enough to Know You
35. A Church Loving God...Touching Lives
36. A Church Making a Difference
37. A Church of Joy
38. A Church of Joy in Jesus
39. A Church of Open Minds, Open Hearts, Open Hands

40. A Church of Welcome, Grace, and Love
41. A Church on the Move Where Involvement is Emphasized
42. A Church that Breaks the Mold
43. A Church that Feels Like Home
44. A Church that is Affirming, Belonging, Caring
45. A Church Where Christians Are Growing
46. A Church Where Christ is the Center of Attention
47. A Church Where First Things Come First
48. A Church Where Friends Become Family
49. A Church Where God is Our Source
50. A Church Where God is Seen, Love is Felt, and Lives are Changed
51. A Church Where it's a Relationship, Not a Religion
52. A Church Where Jesus is Real
53. A Church Where People Really Matter
54. A Church Where the Sermons Make Sense
55. A Church Where the Bible is Taught Verse By Verse
56. A Church Where Time is Well Spent
57. A Church Where You Can Be Liked, Have Fun, Be Challenged and Encouraged
58. A Church Where Your Spiritual Life Can Be As Real And As Useful As You Are
59. A Church With a Dynamic Present and a Future as Bright in the Presence of God
60. A Church With a Friendly Welcome
61. A Church With a Heart
62. A Church With a Heavenly View
63. A Church With a Heavenly Vow
64. A Church With a Purpose
65. A Church With a Song
66. A Church With a Vision
67. A Church With a Vision and a Heart for the Community
68. A Church With a Vision, Leading Humanity to Eternal Life
69. A Church With a Vision to Change a City
70. A Church With Hope
71. A Church With Open Hearts, Open Arms
72. A Church With Strong Family Influence
73. A Church With The Timeless Message of Jesus for the Language of Today
74. A Church-centered Person. A People-centered Passion
75. A City Church With a Purpose
76. A City-Wide Church with a World-Wide Ministry
77. A Comfortable Atmosphere Where Needs are Met Dedicated to Making Christ Known
78. A Community of Faith, Hope, and Charity
79. A Community of Faith Where Thinking Minds and Caring Hearts Can Truly Grow
80. A Community of Faith Works

81. A Community of Good Stewards
82. A Community of Hope
83. A Community of Spirit-filled Believers
84. A Complete Church Program for the Whole Family
85. A Congregation in Renewal
86. A Conservative Congregation with Traditional Worship Service
87. A Contemporary, Casual, Non-Threatening Place to Belong
88. A Contemporary Christian Church Building Community Through Small Groups
89. A Contemporary Church Presenting Historic Christianity
90. A Dispensational Church Studying the Word Rightly Divided
91. A Diverse Community Unified
92. A Family Centered Church
93. A Family Church, Building the Family of God
94. A Family Church Dedicated to Restoring, Renewing, and Relaxing God's People
95. A Family Church With a World Mission
96. A Family Friendly Fellowship
97. A Family of Believers Committed to Reaching People with the Life-Changing Reality of Jesus Christ
98. A Family of Friendly Folks
99. A Family Growing in God's Spirit
100. A Family Worship Center with a Vision for Reaching the World
101. A Friendly Church that Cares About People
102. A Friendly Church with a Loving Savior
103. A Friendly Church with a Vital Message
104. A Friendly Family of Faith
105. A Friendly, Fervent, Fundamental Church
106. A Friendly, Spiritual, and Caring Place to Attend Church
107. A Friend to Man, the Church with a Challenge
108. A Gathering Place for People for People Who Want to Become
109. A Going Church for a Coming Christ
110. A Going Church for a Coming Lord
111. A Going Church for a Coming Savior
112. A Great Church with a Bold Mission
113. A Great Place to Celebrate Jesus
114. A Great Place to Rediscover Your Faith
115. A Growing Church for a Changing World
116. A Growing Church for a Growing Area Standing on the Edge of Tomorrow
117. A Harbor of Rest for the Weary
118. A Home of Old Time Religion
119. A Joyful, Open Community of Seekers
120. A Liberal Religious Community Where Faith and Reason Meet
121. A Life-changing Experience
122. A Light in Our Community
123. A Lord's Church with a World Vision

124. A Loving, Bible-Believing Church
125. A Loving Church Celebrating the Loving God
126. A Loving Word Fellowship Church
127. A Ministry for the Whole Family
128. A Ministry that Can Be Trusted
129. A Mission for Every Member a Challenge
130. A New Church With an Old Message
131. A New Testament Church in Action
132. A New Testament Family of Believers
133. A Non-denominational Bible Teaching Church, Working To Preserve the Home and Family
134. A Peace with Justice Congregation
135. A Pentecostal Church for THIS Generation
136. A People Rooted in God is Word Serving to God's World
137. A People with a Vision
138. A Place for Friendship, for Learning, for Enrichment, for Service, for Worship
139. A Place For Healing Hurts & Building Dreams
140. A Place for New Beginnings
141. A Place for Refuge in a Stormy World
142. A Place of All Ages and Stages
143. A Place of Love and Acceptance
144. A Place of Warmth, Acceptance, and Encouragement
145. A Place to Begin...A Place to Belong
146. A Place to Begin...A Place to Grow
147. A Place to Begin...Belong...Become
148. A Place to Begin; Your Place to Belong
149. A Place to Believe, to Become, to Belong
150. A Place to Belong...A Place to Become
151. A Place to Call Home
152. A Place to Experience the Transforming Love of Christ
153. A Place to Extend Your Family
154. A Place to Find Meaning...A Place to Belong
155. A Place to Love and Be Loved
156. A Place to Make Friends
157. A Place Where Everybody Knows Your Name
158. A Place Where Everyone is Special and Jesus Christ is Lord
159. A Place Where Love is Found
160. A Place Where People Can Glow in His Love, Grow for His Word, and Go in His Power
161. A Place Where Youth Are Important
162. A Place you Can Call Home
163. A Positive Faith Ministry
164. A Practical Friendly Church
165. A Progressive Bible and Christ Centered Church
166. A Real Ministry With a Real Message to a Real People
167. A Reconciling Congregation

168. A Safe Place for Children to Learn
169. A Safe Place to Turn to God at Your Own Pace
170. A Spirited Growth Center
171. A Spirit-Filled Fellowship Where Jesus Christ and His Word Are Both Present and Exalted
172. A Vibrant Church with a Biblical Message
173. A Warm and Caring Church Where All Are Welcome
174. A Warm Friendly Place For You
175. A Warm Supportive Fellowship That Cares About Individuals, Families, and the Community
176. A World of Care Right In Your Neighborhood
177. A Worshipping Family of the King
178. Abiding Word Church
179. Alive Together in Christ
180. All the Gospel for All the People
181. Anchored to the Rock, Geared to the Times
182. An Evangelic Fellowship
183. An Exciting and Friendly Place to Worship
184. An Exciting, Non-Denominational, Interracial Church
185. An Intentionally Integrated Shared Ministry
186. An Oasis of Faith, Hope, and Love
187. An Oasis of Love Family Center
188. An Old Fashioned Baptist Church
189. An Old Fashioned Church Where the SHOUT Has Not Died Out
190. An Open Door is Christian Love
191. Bible Based...Christ Centered...Missions Minded
192. Bible Fed, Spirit Led
193. Bible Teaching For Everyday Living
194. Bound Together for Love
195. Called to Make a Difference
196. Called to Worship...Commissioned to Serve
197. Christ Centered...Bible Based
198. Christ Centered...Care Connected
199. Christ Is the Answer
200. Church and Family Together
201. Church as it Should Be
202. Church in a Whole New Light
203. Church of Tomorrow Here Today
204. Committed to Christ to Care for You
205. Divine People, Inquiring Minds, Open Hearts
206. Exciting Bible-Believing Church
207. Exciting Minister Fulfilling Needs
208. Faithful to the Word of God
209. Family Oriented...Gospel Centered
210. Fast-Growing, Soul-Winning Church
211. Fellowship of Love
212. His People Sharing His Love
213. Home of "Those People At That Church"
214. In a Setting of Love & Friendship in Christ, We Join Together

215. Not Just Another Church, But a Books of Acts Revival
216. People Who Aren't Perfect...and Don't Pretend To Be
217. Practical Christianity in a Friendly Atmosphere
218. Practical Help for Daily Living From the Word of God
219. Sharing the Caring Christ
220. Soul Beaming Lighthouses to the World
221. Spiritual Growth Center
222. The Belonging Place
223. The Church in the Community For the Community
224. The Church Love in Building
225. The Church of Conquerors
226. The Church of Many Faces, One Family
227. The Church on the Cutting Edge
228. The Church On the Way
229. The Church On the Way To Where You Want To Be
230. The Church That Answers the Call of Divinity by Serving Humanity
231. The Church That Cares
232. The Church That Cares the Very Best for Your Soul
233. The Church That Feels Like Home
234. The Church That's Build on Faith
235. The Church That Reaches Up to God, Out to Man
236. The Church That Specializes in Hospitality
237. The Church That Walks By Faith...Not By Sight
238. The Church Where Good Things Always Happen
239. The Church With a Mission, a Message, and a Meaning
240. The Church With a Servant's Heart
241. The Church With a Vision
242. The Church With a Warm Heart
243. The Community of Joy
244. The Enthusiastic Church
245. The Family Church...You're a Part of the Family of God
246. The Family of Faith...Growing in the Light of Christ
247. The Fellowship of Families
248. The Friendly Church For Newcomers, Military, & Tourist Families
249. The Gateway to Life, Meaning, and Purpose Found in Christ
250. The Going Church for the Coming Christ
251. The Love of God Has Made Us a Family
252. The Ministry Meeting the Needs of the Community and Fulfilling the Will of God
253. The Place for New Beginnings
254. The Place for the Entire Family
255. The Place of His Presence
256. The Place to Taste Something Fresh and Exciting
257. The Stairway to Heaven Ministry
258. The Umbrella Church Embracing ALL in Christ
259. The Warm Caring Church With Good Strong Bible Teaching

260. This Body of Believers Exists to Lift Up Jesus Christ and His Teachings to All People
261. Tired of Tradition?...A Church that Breaks the Mold
262. Today's Church...For Today's People
263. We Are an Open and Friendly, Risking, and Caring Community of Faith
264. We Are Christian Only, But Not the Only Christians
265. We Are Here For God and Others
266. We Are More than a Church...We're a Family
267. We Are Real People with Real Needs, Finding Real Answers
268. We Are the Church that Cares About Youth
269. Welcoming Families and Singles Into God's Family
270. Where a Life Changes a Life
271. Where a Warm Welcome Always Awaits Everyone
272. Where Christ is Honored and People are Welcome
273. Where Everybody is Somebody
274. Where Every Visitor is an Honored Servant
275. Where Faith and Life Interact
276. Where Faith Grows and Love Shows
277. Where Faith, Hope, Love Abide
278. Where Faith In Christ Makes You a Member
279. Where Families Matter
280. Where Friends Become Family
281. Where Friendship, Family, and Faith Come Together
282. Where God is Building a Bible Centered Family of Faith
283. Where God is Changing Lives
284. Where God is Healing the Broken Ones
285. Where God is on the Move Changing People's Lives
286. Where God's Old Ways Bring Him Peace
287. Where Heaven and Earth Come Together
288. Where Jesus Christ is Preached in Resurrection Power
289. Where Jesus is Lord and Our Vision is Souls
290. Where Life Comes Together
291. Where Lives are Changed for Christ
292. Where Love Becomes Action
293. Where Love Faith, & Hope Abide
294. Where Love Is
295. Where Love is Paramount and People Gather to Grow
296. Where Love Changes Lives
297. Where Ordinary People Can Experience God
298. Where People Are the Purpose
299. Where People Make a Difference
300. Where Sheep Come to Feed
301. Where Science, Religion, and Life Are Compatible
302. Where Strangers Become Friends
303. Where the Bible and Family Blend
304. Where the Bible Comes Alive

305. Where the Bible is Studied and Taught Without Compromise
306. Where the Living Waters Flow
307. Where the People of God Gather
308. Where the Scriptures Come to Life
309. Where the SON always Shines
310. Where Worship is a Lifestyle
311. Working With Jesus Building His Church
312. Your Transforming Light and Power Company

Slogans: Mission

1. Approaching Faith With Reason, But By Faith Go Beyond Reason
2. Balancing The Truth Of Scripture And The Spirit Of Worship
3. Becoming Disciples Through Faith, Fellowship, Study And Stewardship
4. Believing And Preaching The Word Of God
5. Bible Centered in Message...Christ Centered In Ministry
6. Bonding Our Families With The Love Of Christ
7. Bringing A Merged Relevance Of Making a Difference
8. Bringing Christ To Families
9. Bringing Living Water To A Thirsty World
10. Bringing New Hope
11. Bringing People Together in Worship and Fellowship, and Service
12. Bringing The Church To Destiny
13. Bringing The Family Back Together
14. Bringing The Message Of Love, Acceptance, And Forgiveness Through Jesus Christ
15. Bringing Wholeness Through Jesus Christ
16. Bringing You New Hope In Christ
17. Building Disciplined Followers Of Jesus Christ
18. Building Dreams, Healing Hurts, Helping People Find Greatness In Christ
19. Building God's Kingdom
20. Building God's Kingdom With Love
21. Building Lives For The Future
22. Building Lives To Change The World
23. Building Lives Upon The Word Of God
24. Building Men, Women, & Children Who Will Stand The Test Of Time
25. Building On A Firm Foundation
26. Building On The Same Foundation For Victorious Living
27. Building People Of Destiny
28. Building People Of Integrity
29. Building The Whole Man: Spirit, Body, and Soul
30. Called to Worship...Commissioned to Serve
31. Caring For The Total Person
32. Caring To Send...Sending To Care
33. Celebrating Christ With Unconditional Love
34. Celebrating God's Love, Caring For Others, Communicating Christ
35. Celebrating God's Presence, Communicating God's Word
36. Celebrating Life Through Worship
37. Celebrating The Love Of God
38. Changing Lives To Change The World
39. Christ's Mission Is Our Mission
40. Claiming The Vision That (City, County, World) May Know Jesus

41. Committed To Being God's Alternative To Human Brokenness
42. Committed To Building Healthy Families and Healing Broken Family Relationships
43. Committed To God's Purpose For Your Life
44. Committed To Relevant Bible Teaching
45. Community With the Life Changing Truths of Jesus Christ
46. Compelled By His Love To Change Our World
47. Compelled By Love
48. Continuing The Good Work Of Christ The Good Shepherd
49. Continuing The Work Of Christ, The Good Shepherd
50. Continuing The Work Of Jesus...Peacefully, Simply, Together
51. Developing People for God's Delight
52. Developing People of God's Delight
53. Discovering, Celebrating, and Serving God Together
54. Empowering People
55. Empowering People To Make A Difference
56. Empowering You For Life
57. Encouraging The Study Of God's Word
58. Encouraging, Equipping And Empowering Today's Family
59. Enriching Lives With Christian Love And Truth
60. Equipping Disciples For Service To God's World
61. Equipping Disciples Through Christ's Love
62. Equipping God's People For Ministry
63. Equipping People For The Fullness Of Their Calling
64. Equipping The Saints
65. Equipping The Saints For Ministry In (City) , The Nation, The World
66. Equipping The Saints For The Work Of The Ministry
67. Exalting God & Growing People
68. Exalting Jesus...In the City and to the World
69. Exalting The Lord...Equipping The Saints...Extending The Kingdom
70. Experiencing Calvary's Love
71. Experiencing Christ's Relevance To Our Day-to-Day Lives
72. Experiencing God Together
73. Experiencing God's Love Personally
74. Experiencing The Miraculous Power Of Jesus Christ
75. Experiencing The Power Of The Resurrection
76. Experiencing Together God's Grace And Transforming Power
77. Exploring The Christian Faith In A Relevant And Meaningful Way
78. Expressing The Excitement
79. Extending The Hand Of Jesus To All
80. Fighting For The Cause (Acts 26:18)
81. Fishing For Men And Disciplining Them Is Our Motto
82. Focusing On Christ...Caring For People
83. For The Equipping Of The Saints (Eph 4:12)
84. Fulfilling The Call
85. Gathering In The Name Of Jesus Christ
86. Giving New Meaning To Family

87. Glorifying God And Serving Others
88. Going And Growing With Christ
89. Growing For God's Glory
90. Growing In Spirit...Sharing God's Love
91. Growing In The Knowledge Of Our Salvation
92. Growing To Care...Caring To Grow
93. Growing To Serve
94. Growing Together
95. Growing Together In Faith
96. Growing With A Growth That Is From God (Col. 2:19)
97. Growing With The Glory Of God
98. Healing The Wounded...Training The Warrior
99. Heeding The Word
100. Helping People Find A Positive Relationship With Christ And His Church
101. Helping People Find Hope In Jesus Christ
102. Helping People Find Meaning In Today's World
103. Holding Fast The Faithful Word
104. Holding Forth The Faithful Word...By Sound Doctrine (Titus 1:9)
105. Holding Forth The Word Of Life
106. Impacting The World Through The Love and Power Of God
107. Impacting This Generation For Christ
108. In Pursuit Of The Presence Of God
109. Intersecting Lives With The Love And Life Of Jesus Christ
110. Inviting The Fullness And Liberty Of God's Spirit
111. Joining Hands With Other Churches To Make It Easier To Go To Heaven From (City)
112. Knowing Christ And Serving His Purposes
113. Knowing God
114. Knowing God Is Abundant Life
115. Learning Life's Answers
116. Let's Take The City For Jesus
117. Lifting Up A Standard
118. Living By The Principles As Lived By Jesus Christ
119. Living In Faith Eternally
120. Looking For Life's Answers And Meaningful Relationships
121. Loving God And Loving People
122. Loving God And Serving People
123. Loving God In Front Of People; Loving People In Front Of God
124. Loving God...Serving You
125. Making A Difference in Today's World
126. Making A Difference Through a Balance Of WORSHIP, FELLOWSHIP, & MINSTRY
127. Making Christ Known
128. Making Christian Disciples Who Make Christian Gospels
129. Making Life Even Better
130. Meeting Needs Through God's Love

131. Meeting The Needs Of The Whole Person: Body, Soul, Spirit
132. Meeting The Needs Of Today's Families
133. Ministering A Personal Relationship With Christ Our King
134. Ministering The Joy Of Christ
135. Ministering To All Ages
136. Ministering To All God's People
137. Ministering To Families and Individuals
138. Ministering To Meet All Needs
139. Ministering To The Entire Family
140. Ministering To The Need Of The Whole Family
141. Ministering To Your Needs
142. Ministry That Keeps You Active In Life And Your Community
143. Moving Forward With Christ
144. Offering The Serenity Of Christ For A Changing World
145. Our Mission Is People
146. Pointing People In A New Direction
147. Praising The Name Of Jesus
148. Preaching Christ—Our Only Hope
149. Preaching God's Infallible Word To The Whole Family
150. Preaching God's Love, Acceptance, And Forgiveness
151. Preaching That Makes Sense...Please Join Us
152. Preaching The Doctrine Of Grace
153. Preaching The Lord Jesus Christ—Crucified, Risen, And Coming Again
154. Preaching The Suffering Of Christ
155. Preaching The Truth With Love
156. Preparing Families For The 21st Century
157. Preparing Followers Of Christ For The 21st Century
158. Presenting Ageless Truth In A Contemporary Fashion
159. Presenting Christ To Families
160. Presenting Good News Of Jesus Christ In Word, Song, And Teaching
161. Proclaiming a Great God
162. Proclaiming Christ Alone
163. Proclaiming Christ And Him Crucified
164. Proclaiming God's Grace And Serving Him In Gratitude
165. Proclaiming God's Purpose For Lives
166. Proclaiming God's Word For Today's World
167. Proclaiming Good News From God's Word
168. Proclaiming Justice By Grace, Through Faith Alone
169. Proclaiming The Good News Through Word, Music, And Diction
170. Proclaiming The Gospel For_____Years
171. Proclaiming The Gospel Of God's Sovereign Grace In Christ
172. Proclaiming the Hope of Christ For All People
173. Proclaiming The King And His Kingdom
174. Proclaiming The Truth In Love
175. Providing Life Changing Encounters With God

176. Reaching Hearts With The Holy Spirit
177. Reaching Out For The Savior
178. Reaching Out...Welcoming In...Walking Together
179. Reaching The Lost...Teaching The Saved To Serve
180. Reaching Through Teaching
181. Reaching Up In Worship...Reaching Out In Service
182. Reaching Up...Reaching Out...Reaching For
183. Reaching, Preaching, Teaching
184. Reaching, Touching, Teaching, Changing
185. Restoring New Testament Christianity
186. Restoring The Brokenhearted, Healing The Wounded
187. Rightly Dividing The Word
188. Rising Up To Do The Impossible
189. Seeking God, Serving The Community, Supporting Each Other
190. Seeking The Lord For Christ (Matt 28:19-20)
191. Seeking The Way, Experiencing God's Love, Sharing Our Life
192. Serving A Risen Savior
193. Serving Christ And Neighbor
194. Serving Christ And One Another
195. Serving Christ And The Community Since ______
196. Serving The Lord, Rejoicing In Hope
197. Serving Together In God's Family
198. Sharing a Caring Christ Through Caring People
199. Sharing Christ With The Nations
200. Sharing Christ's Love For Our Community
201. Sharing Faith And Love
202. Sharing God's Love
203. Sharing God's Love, Peace and Forgiveness
204. Sharing God's Peace and Forgiveness
205. Sharing Hope, Faith, Love
206. Sharing Not Only The Gospel, But Our Lives As Well.
207. Sharing That Great Hope
208. Sharing The Good News Worshipping Him
209. Sharing The Heart Of The Gospel In The Heart Of (city)
210. Sharing The Joy Of Christ
211. Sharing The Life, Love, and Laughter Of Jesus Christ
212. Sharing The Love Of Christ
213. Sharing The Promise Of Eternal Life
214. Sharing The Truth In Love
215. Sharing The Truth Inherent In All Great Spiritual Transactions
216. Showing From The Scriptures Salvation Through The Savior
217. Showing Jesus to The World
218. Solid Bible Teaching
219. Speaking The Truth For Love
220. Specializing In New Believers and Young Families
221. Standing Fast In The Faith
222. Still Holding To The Inspired, Infallible Word Of God

223. Still Preaching The Gospel
224. Still Preaching The Old Fashioned Gospel
225. Strengthening Families
226. Strengthening Families Through God's Love
227. Strengthening The Family
228. Teaching A Christ-centered Way Of Life
229. Teaching and Applying God's Word
230. Teaching God's Word Verse By Verse
231. Teaching The Bible To Learn...Applying The Bible To Grow
232. Teaching The Bible To Touch People With God's Love
233. Teaching The Uncompromised Word Of Faith For The Challenges Of Today
234. Teaching The Word With Understanding
235. Teaching The Word...Flowing With The Spirit
236. Teaching The Word...Reaching The World
237. Teaching Traditional Values
238. The Whole Message For The Whole World
239. To Awaken Humanity To Its Spiritual Magnificence
240. To Bring Love, Miracles, & Spiritual Awareness To Everyday Life
241. To Develop a Biblically Functioning Community That Impacts our Surrounding
242. To Enjoy The Lord Forever
243. To Glorify God, To Make Disciples Of Jesus Christ, To Grow In Love
244. To Herald The Coming Of Christ
245. To Honor God By Making Disciples and Teaching Them to Love God and People
246. To Know God And Make Him Known
247. To Know Him...To Make Him Known
248. To Know Jesus Christ as Friend, Savior, and Lord, and to Make Him Known
249. Touching Lives For Now And Eternity
250. Touching Lives With Christ's Love
251. Trained In Truth, Touching The World
252. Transforming Lives...Building Christian Character
253. Uniting Believers For Christ
254. Vibrantly Alive For Christ And The World
255. We Care About People
256. We Preach Christ Crucified
257. We're Building Lives On God's Wordh
258. Welcoming Families and Singles Into God's Friendship
259. Where Love Is Released And Faith Is Increased
260. Winning The Lost...Training The Saved
261. Working To Gather
262. Working Together...Caring For The World
263. Working With Jesus Building His Church
264. Worshipping The Lord, Teaching The Scripture, Releasing The Power Of The Holy Spirit, Sharing Christ's Love

Slogans: Invitational

1. A Church Alive Is Worth The Drive
2. A Church Large Enough To Serve You And Small Enough To Know You
3. A Complete Church Program For Your Whole Family
4. A Friendly, Caring Church That Cares About You
5. A Great Place To Rediscover Your Faith
6. A Place For You
7. A Place Where Friends Become Family
8. A Warm Welcome Awaits You
9. A Warm, Friendly Place For You
10. Alive To Your Needs
11. An Extension Of God's Love For You
12. Are You Turned Off To Religion, But Not To God?
13. Baby Boomers - Look, A Church Designed For You
14. Change Your Thinking...Change Your Life
15. Changing The Way You Think About Church
16. Christ's Family Inventing Your Family
17. Church Doesn't Have To Be Boring
18. Come And Experience The Presence Of God
19. Come and Learn Life's Answers
20. Come and Let Jesus Happen To You
21. Come as a Visitor—Stay as a Friend.
22. Come As You Are - You'll Be Loved
23. Come As You Are And Follow Jesus With Us
24. Come Celebrate Jesus With Us
25. Come Expecting A Miracle
26. Come Expecting Sound Doctrine, Spirited Music, Positive Preaching, Exuberant Worship
27. Come Share The Spirit
28. Come To The Growing Church
29. Come Visit Us In Our New Building
30. Come Worship With Us; Rejoice To The Lord
31. Come, Grow With Us
32. Committed To God's Purpose For Your Life
33. Discover A Whole New World
34. Discover The Difference
35. Enjoy The Difference
36. Enter To Worship...Leave To Serve
37. Expect A Miracle Christ
38. Experience Celebration Form The Heart

39. Experience New Life
40. Experience The Excitement
41. Experience The Extraordinary
42. Experience The Grace Of God And The Joy Of Christ With Us
43. Experience The Joy
44. Family Oriented—Gospel Centered
45. Find Connection And Commentary With Us
46. Find God's Love Among People Who Care
47. Find Yourself And Jesus
48. Get Back In Touch With The God You Once Knew
49. God Can Help
50. Here Is Your Opportunity
51. Hurting People Welcomed Here
52. Isn't It Time For Jesus?
53. It's Time To Come Home
54. It's Worth The Drive
55. Join Our Growing Family
56. Join Us As We Celebrate God's Love For Us
57. Join Us Sunday For ______________
58. Large Enough To Reach You...Small Enough To Touch You
59. Looking For A Church That Embraces Sound Values And Preaches A Message Of Hope?
60. Looking For a Church That Preaches the Word?
61. Looking for a Church That Will Care For You Like Family?
62. Looking For A Warm, Friendly Church?
63. New Residents Welcome
64. Newcomers Welcome
65. Our Church Can Be Your Home
66. Our Promise - A Warm Welcome, Relevant Messages, Quality Child-care, No Pleas For Money
67. Reaching Out To You
68. Return To New Testament Christianity
69. Share In The Joy Of Worship And Revival
70. Skeptics And Newcomers Welcome
71. Stop Awhile and Rest Here (Gen. 18:4)
72. The Church Small Enough To Know You & Large Enough To Serve You
73. The End Of Your Search For A Friendly Church
74. The Place For the Entire Family
75. The Word Will Change Your Life
76. There Are No Strangers Here, Only Friends You Haven't Met Yet
77. This Is The Way, Walk Us In It
78. Tired Of Traditional Church ?
79. Tough Week? We're Open On Sundays
80. Try It God's Way
81. Try It...You'll Like It
82. Visitors Expected

83. We Care...Come And See
84. We Give You Hope
85. We Love Visitors
86. We Love You Just The Way You Are
87. We Want You To Know That God Loves You
88. We're Always Expecting Company
89. Welcome To The Family Of God Centered On His Word
90. Where Faith In Christ Makes You A Member
91. Where You Can Learn About God And Make New Friends
92. Whosoever Will May Come
93. Why Not Attend One of Our Services This Week?
94. Worship Him In Spirit And In Truth
95. You Are One, You'll Come Again
96. You Are Welcome, Whether In Your Best Suit or Most Comfortable Jeans
97. You Make The Difference
98. You'll Be Glad You Found Time To Worship With Us
99. You'll Love The Difference
100. You're Never A Stranger In Your Father's House
101. Your Next Step

Churches Visited

CHURCHES VISITED

1.	Abundant Life Assembly	Cupertino, CA	4-18-99
2.	Abundant Life Church	Menlo Park, CA	1-17-99
3.	Abundant Life Fellowship	Hayward, CA	9-22-96
4.	Abundant Life United Holy Church of America	Alexandria, VA	7-02-00
5.	Advent of Christ the King Church	San Francisco, CA	5-07-00
6.	Agape Community Church	San Pablo, CA	11-22-98
7.	Airport Church of Christ	So. San Francisco, CA	5-07-00
8.	Alamo Christian Assembly Church	Alamo, CA	4-30-00
9.	All Saints Catholic Church	Hayward, CA	9-21-97
10.	Allen Temple Baptist Church	Oakland, CA	10-27-96
11.	Almaden Neighborhood Church	San Jose, CA	6-04-00
12.	Amador Valley Christian Fellowship	Dublin, CA	6-28-98
13.	Amazing Grace Methodist Church	Olathe, KS	7-17-99
14.	Amos Temple CME Church	Oakland, CA	4-20-97
15.	Ananda Church of Self Realization	Palo Alto, CA	4-11-99
16.	Antioch Progressive Baptist Church	Sacramento, CA	6-07-98
17.	Apostles Lutheran Church	San Jose, CA	2-08-98
18.	Apostolic Church of Faith	San Francisco, CA	2-02-97
19.	Apostolic Faith Church	Hayward, CA	4-12-98
20.	Aquarium Foundation Spiritualist Church	San Francisco, CA	7-04-99
21.	Ashbury Methodist Chapel	Livermore, CA	3-29-98
22.	Ashland Freewill Baptist Church	Hayward, CA	3-12-00
23.	Assembly Apostolic Church	Santa Clara, CA	9-08-96
24.	Assembly of God Church	San Bruno, CA	10-06-96
25.	Assembly of God Community Church	San Francisco, CA	5-24-98
26.	Baptist G.A.R.B. Church	San Jose, CA	8-17-97
27.	Bascilia Church	Washington, D.C	7-03-00
28.	Bay Area Baptist Church	Newark, CA	10-06-96
29.	Bay Area Bible Fellowship	Hayward, CA	10-18-98
30.	Bay Hills Community Church	Hayward, CA	3-23-97
31.	Berean Baptist Church	Fremont, CA	5-14-00
32.	Beth Eden Church	Oakland, CA	4-20-97
33.	Bethany Presbyterian	San Bruno, CA	7-26-98
34.	Bethel AMC Church	San Francisco, CA	10-25-98
35.	Bethel Baptist Church	Fremont, CA	12-29-96
36.	Bethel Christian Church	San Francisco, CA	11-03-96
37.	Bethel Church	Modesto, CA	6-19-99
38.	Bethel Church	San Jose, CA	4-23-00
39.	Bethel Family Church	Livermore, CA	4-25-99
40.	Bethel Lutheran Church	Cupertino, CA	4-09-00
41.	Bethel Temple	Hayward, CA	2-22-98
42.	Bethlehem Lutheran Church	Oakland, CA	3-30-97

43. Bethlehem Lutheran Church Santa Rosa, CA 5-09-99
44. Bethlehem Lutheran Church Berkeley, CA 8-27-00
45. Bochasanwasi Si Swaminaregan Sanstha-Hindu Temple Milpitas, CA 9-12-99
46. Broadmoor Community Church San Leandro, CA 6-07-99
47. Broadmore Presbyterian Church Daly City, CA 10-10-99
48. Calvary Armenian Congregational Church San Francisco, CA 9-07-97
49. Calvary Baptist Hayward, CA 10-05-97
50. Calvary Baptist Church Lenexa, KS 7-25-99
51. Calvary Baptist Church, San Francisco, CA 8-22-99
52. Calvary Chapel Sacramento, CA 2-23-97
53. Calvary Chapel (Baptist) Los Gatos, CA 7-11-99
54. Calvary Christian Center Alameda, CA 9-20-98
55. Calvary Lutheran Church Millbrae, CA 2-07-99
56. Calvary Lutheran Church San Lorenzo, CA 2-22-98
57. Calvary Presbyterian Church Berkeley, CA 10-20-96
58. Calvary Presbyterian Church San Francisco, CA 8-09-98
59. Calvary Temple Assembly of God Church San Leandro, CA 1-12-97
60. Calvary Temple Modesto, CA 6-20-99
61. Calvary United Methodist Church San Francisco, CA 2-09-97
62. Calvary Worship Center Burnaby, B.C. 8-01-99
63. Canaan Covenant Baptist Church Oakland, CA 12-22-96
64. Canyon Creek Presbyterian Church San Ramon, CA 8-31-97
65. Cathedral of Faith San Jose, CA 12-15-96
66. Cathedral of St. John Providence RI 7-12-98
67. Cathedral of the Immaculate Conception Kansas City, MO 7-24-99
68. Cedar Boulevard Neighborhood Church Newark, CA 7-13-97
69. Cedar Grove Community Church Livermore, CA 4-25-99
70. Celebration Christian Center Livermore, CA 7-16-00
71. Centenary United Methodist Modesto, CA 6-20-99
72. Centerville Presbyterian Church Fremont, CA 5-04-97
73. Central Baptist Church Alameda, CA 5-03-98
74. Central Baptist Church Hermleigh, TX 10-22-99
75. Central Peninsula Church Foster City, CA 5-31-98
76. Central United Methodist Church Sacramento, CA 6-07-98
77. Central United Methodist Church Stockton, CA 6-01-97
78. Chinese Bible Fellowship Danville, CA 12-12-99
79. Chinese Church Menlo Park, CA 1-12-97
80. Chinese Mennonite Church Vancouver, B.C. 8-01-99
81. Christ Church Alexandria, VA 7-02-00
82. Christ Church San Mateo, CA 9-12-99
83. Christ Community Church Hayward, CA 1-08-98

84. Christ Lutheran Church	El Cerrito, CA	5-03-98
85. Christ Lutheran Church	San Francisco, CA	2-09-97
86. Christ Presbyterian Church	San Leandro, CA	1-16-00
87. Christ the King Church	Campbell, CA	11-21-99
88. Christ the King Lutheran Church	Fremont, CA	5-14-00
89. Christ's Community Church	Hayward, CA	1-08-98
90. Christ's Episcopal Church	Overland Park, KS	7-18-99
91. Christadelphia Church	San Mateo, CA	4-18-99
92. Christian Cathedral	Oakland, CA	8-18-96
93. Christian Church	Fremont, CA	7-13-97
94. Christian Church	Santa Clara, CA	9-08-96
95. Christian Community Church	San Jose, CA	3-01-98
96. Christian Life Center	Hayward, CA	4-28-96
97. Christian Life Fellowship	Sacramento, CA	2-23-97
98. Christian Reformed Church	San Jose, CA	11-21-99
99. Christian Tabernacle	Hayward, CA	1-08-98
100.Christian World Ministries	Livermore, CA	11-07-99
101.Church at Mission Peak	Fremont, CA	4-19-98
102.Church Mount of Blessing	Hayward, CA	9-19-97
103.Church of Christ	Milpitas, CA	6-28-98
104.Church of Christ	Santa Rosa, CA	5-09-99
105.Church of Christ	Hayward,CA	9-03-00
106.Church of Christ	Pleasanton, CA	2-27-00
107.Church of Christ	San Lorenzo, CA	1-30-00
108.Church of Christ, Industrial Parkway	Hayward, CA	6-18-00
109.Church of God of Prophecy	Castro Valley, CA	12-15-96
110.Church of Jesus Christ (LDS)	Sunnyvale, CA	9-05-99
111.Church of the Cross	Modesto, CA	11-28-99
112.Church of the Highlands	San Bruno, CA	7-26-98
113.Church of the Incarnation	Santa Rosa, CA	5-09-99
114.Church of the Valley	San Ramon, CA	4-16-00
115.Clayton Valley Church	Concord, CA	12-19-99
116.College Ave. Congregational United	Church of Christ	
	Modesto, CA	11-08-98
117.Community Baptist Church	Hayward, CA	7-01-97
118.Community Church	Pleasanton, CA	8-10-97
119.Community Church of Hayward	Hayward, CA	9-01-96
120.Community Church	Brisbane, CA	9-12-99
121.Community House of Prayer	Los Gatos, CA	7-11-99
122.Community Methodist Church	Millbrae, CA	10-17-99
123.Community Presbyterian Church	Danville, CA	3-19-00
124.Condon Street Baptist Church	Providence RI	7-12-98
125.Congregational Church	Redwood City, CA	3-09-97
126.Congregational Church	San Mateo, CA	5-11-97
127.Congregational Church	Danville, CA	12-12-99
128.Corinthian Baptist Church	Oakland, CA	6-29-97
129.Cornerstone Apostolic Church	Hayward, CA	9-07-97

130.Cornerstone Church	San Francisco, CA	6-08-97
131.Cornerstone Fellowship	Livermore, CA	4-25-99
132.Covenant Orthodox Presbyterian Church	Berkeley, CA	10-25-97
133.Creekside Community Church	Alamo, CA	4-30-00
134.Crossroads Church	Fremont, CA	6-27-99
135.Crosswinds Church	Dublin, CA	1-19-97
136.Downs Memorial United Methodist Church	Oakland, CA	8-27-00
137.Dublin Christian Church	Dublin, CA	1-19-97
138.East Bay Church of Religious Science	Oakland, CA	9-15-96
139.East Bay Faith Center	Hayward, CA	12-22-96
140.East Side Church of Christ	Snyder, TX	10-24-99
141.East Side Church of God In Christ	San Jose, CA	8-17-97
142.East Valley Church	San Jose, CA	11-21-99
143.Eden United Church of Christ	Hayward, CA	11-15-98
144.Elmhurst Baptist Church	Hayward, CA	5-05-96
145.Epiphany Lutheran Church	San Leandro, CA	5-02-99
146.Episcopal Church in Almaden	San Jose, CA	6-04-00
147.Eternal Sacred Order of Cherubum and Seraphim	Hayward, CA	9-19-97
148.Evangel Christian Fellowship	San Jose, CA	8-13-00
149.Evangelical Free Church	Newark, CA	6-21-98
150.Evangelical Free Church	Oakland, CA	6-30-96
151.Evangelical Free Church	Pleasanton, CA	8-06-00
152.Fairway Park Baptist Church	Hayward, CA	12-26-99
153.Faith Chapel Assembly of God	Pleasanton, CA	1-04-98
154.Faith Fellowship	San Leandro, CA	1-31-99
155.Faith Lutheran Church	Castro Valley, CA	6-23-96
156.Faith Lutheran Church	Prairie Village, KS	7-18-99
157.Faith Restoration Fellowship	Hayward, CA	2-06-00
158.Faith Romanian Church	Hayward, CA	8-02-98
159.Faith United Methodist Church	Sacramento, CA	6-07-98
160.Faith United Methodist Church	San Leandro, CA	2-28-99
161.Family Community Church	San Jose, CA	2-08-98
162.Fellowship Bible Church	Belmont, CA	3-26-00
163.First Apostolic Church	San Leandro, CA	6-13-99
164.First Assembly of God Church	Fremont, CA	11-10-96
165.First Assembly of God Church	Snyder, TX	10-24-99
166.First Baptist Church	Alameda, CA	11-09-97
167.First Baptist Church	Berkeley, CA	3-24-96
168.First Baptist Church	Castro Valley, CA	4-21-96
169.First Baptist Church	Dublin, CA	12-06-98
170.First Baptist Church	Menlo Park, CA	3-02-97
171.First Baptist Church	Milpitas, CA	2-14-99
172.First Baptist Church	Modesto, CA	11-08-98

173.First Baptist Church	Napa, CA	5-16-99
174.First Baptist Church	Oakland, CA	6-29-97
175.First Baptist Church	Pleasanton, CA	7-26-98
176.First Baptist Church	Rohnert Park, CA	5-09-99
177.First Baptist Church	San Francisco, CA	4-06-97
178.First Baptist Church	San Jose, CA	6-22-97
179.First Baptist Church	San Lorenzo, CA	9-05-96
180.First Baptist Church	San Mateo, CA	12-21-97
181.First Baptist Church	Sunnyvale, CA	7-28-96
182.First Baptist Church of America	Providence RI	7-12-98
183.First Baptist Church of San Lorenzo Valley	Felton, CA	11-30-97
184.First Baptist Church	Daly City, CA	8-29-99
185.First Baptist Church	Hermleigh, TX	10-22-99
186.First Baptist Church	Kansas City, MO	7-25-99
187.First Baptist Church	Los Altos, CA	12-05-99
188.First Baptist Church	Sacramento, CA	8-20-00
189.First Baptist Church	San Carlos, CA	3-26-00
190.First Baptist Church	San Rafael, CA	6-11-00
191.First Baptist Church	Snyder, TX	10-24-9
192.First Baptist Church	Vancouver, B.C.	8-01-99
193.First Christian Church	Castro Valley, CA	4-11-98
194.First Christian Church	Hayward, CA	9-06-98
195.First Christian Church	Napa, CA	5-16-99
196.First Christian Church	San Lorenzo, CA	1-30-00
197.First Christian Reformed	Modesto, CA	6-20-99
198.First Church of Christ Scientist	Hayward, CA	7-02-97
199.First Church of God	Ira, TX	10-21-99
200.First Covenant Church	Oakland, CA	12-22-96
201.First Covenant Church	San Francisco, CA	6-08-97
202.First Nazarene Church	Vallejo, CA	9-03-00
203.First Presbyterian Church	Alameda, CA	3-28-99
204.First Presbyterian Church	Berkeley, CA	5-12-96
205.First Presbyterian Church	Burlingame, CA	7-26-98
206.First Presbyterian Church	Hayward, CA	4-21-96
207.First Presbyterian Church	Livermore, CA	3-29-98
208.First Presbyterian Church	Miami, Fl.	11-23-97
209.First Presbyterian Church	Milpitas, CA	3-21-99
210.First Presbyterian Church	Newark, CA	4-13-97
211.First Presbyterian Church	San Leandro, CA	6-16-96
212.First Presbyterian Church	San Mateo, CA	l-10-99
213.First Presbyterian Church	Stockton, CA	6-01-97
214.First Presbyterian Church	Concord, CA	6-25-00
215.First Presbyterian Church	Palo Alto, CA	3-05-00
216.First Presbyterian Church	Santa Clara, CA	2-20-00
217.First Presbyterian Church	Sunnyvale, CA	12-05-99
218.First Presbyterian Church	Vallejo, CA	9-03-00

219.First Spiritualistic Temple	San Francisco, CA	10-25-98
220.First Tabernacle Church	Sacramento, CA	6-07-98
221.First Unitarian Univeralist Church	San Francisco, CA	10-12-97
222.First United Methodist Church	Hayward, CA	3-08-98
223.First United Methodist Church	Campbell, CA	4-23-00
224.First United Methodist Church	Castro Valley, CA	2-06-00
225.First United Methodist Church	San Leandro, CA	2-06-00
226.First United Presbyterian Church	San Francisco, CA	9-07-97
227.Foothill Baptist Church	Castro Valley, CA	6-14-98
228.Foothill Community Church	Santa Rosa, CA	5-09-99
229.Foothill Covenant Church	Los Altos, CA	4-09-00
230.Foursquare Church	Napa, CA	5-16-99
231.Freewill Baptist Church	Antioch, CA	4-27-97
232.Fremont Bible Fellowship	Fremont, CA	6-27-99
233.Fremont Community Church	Fremont, CA	5-26-96
234.Fremont Evangelical Church	Fremont, CA	6-02-96
235.Fruitvale Presbyterian Church	Oakland, CA	11-01-98
236.Full Faith Church of Love	Shawnee, KS	7-25-99
237.Full Gospel Temple	Hayward, CA	8-04-96
238.Gateway Community Church	San Jose, CA	6-22-97
239.Gethsemane Community Church	Berkeley, CA	5-18-97
240.Glad Tidings Assembly	San Francisco, CA	2-02-97
241.Glad Tidings Church	Hayward, CA	4-04-99
242.Glide Memorial Methodist Church	San Francisco, CA	4-06-97
243.Gnostic Church	Palo Alto, CA	12-28-97
244.Good Shepherd Community Church	Tracy, CA	5-30-99
245.Good Shepherd Lutheran Church	Concord, CA	1-24-99
246.Good Shepherd Lutheran Church	Hayward, CA	5-28-00
247.Gospel Lighthouse	San Lorenzo, CA	7-07-96
248.Grace and Holy Trinity Cathedral	Kansas City, MO	7-25-99
249.Grace Baptist Church	Fremont, CA	4-19-98
250.Grace Baptist Church	Tracy, CA	5-30-99
251.Grace Cathedral	San Francisco, CA	11-07-99
252.Grace Church	Pleasanton, CA	1-23-00
253.Grace Fellowship Community Church	Hayward, CA	8-11-96
254.Grace Lutheran Church	Palo Alto, CA	1-26-97
255.Grace Lutheran Church	Pittsburg, CA	4-27-97
256.Grace Lutheran	Hayward, CA	9-26-99
257.Grace United Methodist Church	San Ramon, CA	5-10-98
258.Greater Power House Church	Santa Rosa, CA	5-09-99
259.Greek Orthodox Church	Oakland, CA	6-09-96
260.Halcyon Baptist Church	San Leandro, CA	4-16-00
261.Hamilton Square Baptist Church	San Francisco, CA	3-23-97
262.Harvest Church	Concord, CA	1-24-99
263.Harvest Valley Christian	Pleasanton, CA	10-03-99
264.Hayward Foursquare Church	Hayward, CA	5-30-99

265.Hayward Seventh Day Adventist Church		
	Hayward, CA	3-20-99
266.Hessel Church	Sebastopal, CA	5-23-99
267.High Street Presbyterian Church	Oakland, CA	3-07-97
268.Highland Baptist Church	Hayward, CA	2-25-96
269.Hillcrest Covenant	Prairie Village, KS	7-18-99
270.Hillsdale United Methodist Church	San Mateo, CA	1-10-99
271.Hillside Church of Marin	Corte Madera, CA	3-07-99
272.Hillside Covenant Church	Walnut Creek, CA	8-15-99
273.Hilltop Community Church	Richmond, CA	12-20-97
274.Holy Cross Lutheran	Concord, CA	9-19-99
275.Holy Innocents Episcopal Church	San Francisco, CA	11-10-96
276.Holy Spirit Catholic Church	Fremont, CA	5-21-00
277.Holy Trinity Cathedral	San Francisco, CA	7-30-00
278.Holy Trinity Lutheran Church	Fremont, CA	5-14-00
279.Hope Lutheran Church	San Mateo, CA	2-29-98
280.Hope Lutheran Church	Santa Clara, CA	9-08-96
281.Hope Lutheran Church	Daly City, CA	8-29-99
282.House of Prayer	Newark, CA	5-24-98
283.Immaculate Heart of Mary	Belmont, CA	3-26-00
284.Immanuel Lutheran Church	Los Altos, CA	8-13-00
285.Irvington Baptist Church	Fremont, CA	8-24-97
286.Irvington Presbyterian	Fremont, CA	6-27-99
287.Island United Church	Foster City, CA	5-31-98
288.Japanese Christian Church	San Lorenzo, CA	4-02-99
289.John Knox Presbyterian Church	Dublin, CA	3-28-97
290.Journey Church	Pleasanton, CA	1-23-00
291.Jubilee Christian Center	San Jose, CA	4-04-97
292.Ladera Community Church	Portola Valley, CA	3-05-00
293.Lafayette-Orinda Presbyterian Church		
	Lafayette, CA	8-15-99
294.Lake Merritt United Methodist Church		
	Oakland, CA	4-12-98
295.Lakeshore Avenue Baptist Church	Oakland, CA	11-01-98
296.Lakeview Assembly Church	Stockton, CA	2-13-00
297.Lakewood Village Baptist Church	Sunnyvale, CA	3-21-99
298.LDS Glenmoor Ward	Fremont, CA	6-27-99
299.LDS Headquarters	Independence, MO	7-25-99
300.Lewelling Community Church	San Lorenzo, CA	9-01-96
301.Liberty Christian Fellowship	Fremont, CA	6-10-01
302.Little Flock Church of God	Redwood City, CA	5-11-97
303.Living Hope Assembly Church	San Francisco, CA	11-03-96
304.Lutheran Church of the Cross	Berkeley, CA	5-18-97
305.Lutheran Church of the Holy Spirit	San Francisco, CA	11-03-96
306.Lynnewood Methodist Church	Pleasanton, CA	2-21-99
307.Manor Baptist Church	San Leandro, CA	5-26-96
308.Marin Covenant Church	San Rafael, CA	6-11-00

309.McGee Avenue Baptist Church	Oakland, CA	10-20-96
310.Memorial Tabernacle	Oakland, CA	8-27-00
311.Menlo Park Presbyterian Church	Menlo Park, CA	1-17-99
312.Messiah Lutheran Church	Danville, CA	8-02-98
313.Messiah Lutheran Church	Hayward, CA	1-08-98
314.Metaphysical Church of Enlightenment	Burlingame, CA	5-11-97
315.Metropolitan Community Church	San Francisco, CA	7-13-97
316.Metropolitan Community Church	San Lorenzo, CA	12-15-96
317.Metropolitan Memorial Methodist Church	Washington, D.C.	7-09-00
318.Mission Springs Church	Fremont, CA	2-15-98
319.Missionary Landmark Baptist Church	Hayward, CA	1-16-00
320.Modesto Covenant Church	Modesto, CA	11-08-98
321.Montclair United Methodist Church	Oakland, CA	4-12-98
322.Montclaire Presbyterian Church	Oakland, CA	7-23-00
323.Mount of Olive Lutheran Church	Milpitas, CA	9-08-96
324.Mt. Eden Presbyterian Church	Hayward, CA	8-16-98
325.Mt. Zion Lutheran Church	Richmond, CA	5-18-97
326.Nall Avenue Baptist Church	Overland Park, KS	7-18-99
327.National Presbyterian Church	Washington, D.C	7-09-00
328.Nazarene Church	Antioch, CA	4-27-97
329.Neighborhood Church	Castro Valley, CA	6-23-96
330.Neighborhood Church	Modesto, CA	11-28-99
331.New Dimension Deliverance Center	Hayward, CA	5-28-00
332.New Hope Church	Oakland, CA	5-12-97
333.New Hope Community Church	Fremont, CA	5-21-00
334.New Life Christian Center	North Vancouver, B.C.	8-01-99
335.New Life Christian Fellowship	Castro Valley, CA	3-14-99
336.New Life Christian Fellowship	Petaluma, CA	5-23-99
337.New Life Tabernacle	Napa, CA	5-16-99
338.New Testament Christian Church	San Leandro, CA	5-30-99
339.Newark Christian Center	Newark, CA	3-09-97
340.North Valley Baptist Church	Santa Clara	3-16-97
341.North Valley Christian Fellowship	San Jose, CA	5-25-97
342.Northland Cathedral	Kansas City, MO	7-25-99
343.Northminster Presbyterian Church	El Cerrito, CA	5-03-98
344.Northshore Community Alliance Church	Richmond, CA	11-22-98
345.Oak Grove Baptist Church	San Jose, CA	1-09-00
346.Oak Hill Presbyterian Church	Concord, CA	12-19-99
347.Oak Park Assembly of God	Pleasant Hill, CA	10-31-99
348.Oak Park Christian Center	Pleasant Hill, CA	6-25-00
349.Old First Church	San Francisco, CA	10-13-96
350.Our Lady of Lourdes Church	Arlington, VA	7-03-00
351.Our Lady of Lourdes Church	Oakland, CA	9-04-99

352.Our Lady of Perpetual Help Redemptorist Catholic	Kansas City, MO	7-24-99
353.Our Savior's Lutheran Church	Fremont, CA	4-05-98
354.Our Savior's Lutheran	Livermore, CA	11-07-99
355.Palma Ceia Baptist Church	Hayward, CA	3-15-98
356.Paradise Baptist Church	Oakland, CA	11-17-96
357.Park Boulevard Presbyterian Church	San Leandro, CA	9-21-97
358.Park Street Church	Boston, Mass	7-12-98
359.Parkway Baptist Church	Dublin, CA	6-22-97
360.Peninsula Christian Church	Redwood City, CA	2-16-97
361.Peninsula Covenant Church	Redwood City, CA	3-02-97
362.Piedmont Neighborhood Church	Piedmont, CA	8-18-96
363.Pilgrim Baptist Church	San Mateo, CA	10-17-99
364.Pilgrim Temple	Hayward, CA	3-08-98
365.Pleasant Valley Baptist Church	Liberty, MO	7-22-99
366.Pleasant View Church of Christ	Dublin, CA	11-29-98
367.Presbyterian Community Church	Pleasanton, CA	1-04-98
368.Prince of Peace Church	Fremont, CA	1-24-97
369.Providence Orthodox Presbyterian Church	Hayward, CA	7-11-99
370.Red Bridge United Methodist Church	Kansas City, MO	7-18-99
371.Redeemer Lutheran Church	Redwood City, CA	3-09-97
372.Redwood Baptist Church	Redwood City, CA	12-06-98
373.Redwood Chapel	Castro Valley, CA	4-28-96
374.Redwood Church	Redwood City, CA	2-16-97
375.Redwood Covenant Church	Santa Rosa, CA	5-09-99
376.Religious Science Church	Oakland, CA	12-22-96
377.Rescue Center Baptist Church	Hayward, CA	8-23-98
378.Resurrection Greek Orthodox Church	Castro Valley, CA	3-14-99
379.Resurrection Lutheran Church	Dublin, CA	3-28-99
380.Revival Center	Vallejo, CA	9-03-00
381.River Church Community Church	Sunnyvale, CA	9-05-99
382.RLDS Headquarters	Independence, MO	7-25-99
383.Rolling Hills Community Church	Danville, CA	8-31-97
384.Russian Orthodox Church	San Francisco, CA	5-17-98
385.San Bruno United Methodist Church	San Bruno, CA	4-09-98
386.San Leandro Community Church	San Leandro, CA	5-12-96
387.San Lorenzo Baptist Church	San Lorenzo, CA	4-14-96
388.San Ramon Presbyterian Church	San Ramon, CA	10-05-97
389.San Ramon Valley Bible Church	San Ramon, CA	7-06-97
390.San Ramon Valley United Methodist Church	Alamo, CA	8-08-99

391.Santa Teresa Hills Presbyterian Church San Jose, CA 1-09-00
392.Seaside Baptist Church Pacifica, CA 12-13-98
393.Seeds of Joy Ministries Church of God Modesto, CA 6-20-99
394.Sequoyah Community Church Oakland, CA 12-15-96
395.Seven Trees Baptist Church San Jose, CA 5-25-97
396.Shell Ridge Community Church Walnut Creek, CA 12-29-96
397.Shiloh Christian Fellowship Oakland, CA 5-13-97
398.Shiloh Pentecostal Church Oakland, CA 11-24-96
399.Shinnyo Buddhist Temple Burlingame, CA 6-06-99
400.Skyline Community Church UCC Oakland, CA 4-12-98
401.South Bay Community Church Fremont, CA 7-13-97
402.South Bay ECK Center San Jose, CA 4-24-99
403.South Hills Community Church San Jose, CA 6-04-00
404.Southern Alameda, CA County Buddhist Union City, CA 4-04-99
405.St Mark's Lutheran Church San Francisco, CA 7-30-00
406.St. Alban's Episcopal Church Albany, CA 5-18-96
407.St. Albin's Episcopal Church Lenexa, KS 7-25-99
408.St. Andrew's Presbyterian Church Marin City, CA 3-07-98
409.St. Andrew's Wesley Church Vancouver, BC. 8-01-99
410.St. Antonius Coptic Church Hayward, CA 3-08-98
411.St. Bartholomew's Catholic Church San Mateo, CA 12-21-97
412.St. Catherine of Sienna Church Burlingame, CA 6-06-99
413.St. Christopher's Episcopal Church San Lorenzo, CA 6-29-97
414.St. Claire's Episcopal Church Pleasanton, CA 1-23-00
415.St. Clements Catholic Church Hayward, CA 5-28-00
416.St. Cuthbert's Episcopal Church Oakland, CA 11-17-96
417.St. Edmund's Episcopal Church Pacifica, CA 12-13-98
418.St. Francis Episcopal Church Novato, CA 5-23-99
419.St. Gregory's Episcopal Church San Francisco, CA 11-10-96
420.St. James Lutheran Church San Leandro, CA 1-30-00
421.St. James' Anglican Church Vancouver, B.C. 8-01-99
422.St. James' Episcopal Church Fremont, CA 5-26-96
423.St .James' Episcopal Church San Francisco, CA 5-17-98
424.St. James' Lutheran San Leandro, CA 1-30-00
425.St. John's Lutheran Church Napa, CA 5-16-99
426.St. John's Lutheran Church Sunnyvale, CA 9-05-99
427.St. Joseph's Catholic Church Modesto, CA 11-28-99
428.St. Jude Parish Church San Jose, CA 2-08-98
429.St. Luke's Episcopal Church Los Gatos, CA 7-11-99
430.St. Mark's Episcopal Church Santa Clara, CA 3-16-97
431.St. Mary's Cathedral San Francisco, CA 4-06-97
432.St. Mary's Episcopal Church Napa, CA 5-15-99
433.St. Matthew's Episcopal Church San Mateo, CA 1-04-00

434.St. Michael's Ukrainian Orthodox Church		
	San Francisco, CA	7-19-98
435.St. Paschal Baylon Church	Oakland, CA	3-31-99
436.St. Patrick's Catholic Church	Rodeo, CA	8-07-99
437.St. Paul's Episcopal Church	Burlingame, CA	6-06-99
438.St. Paul's Lutheran Church	Tracy, CA	5-30-99
439.St. Peter's Lutheran Church	Modesto, CA	11-28-99
440.St. Philip's Lutheran Church	Dublin, CA	12-12-99
441.St. Timothy's Episcopal Church	Danville, CA	3-19-00
442.St. Vincent DePaul's Church	San Francisco, CA	8-09-98
443.Starr King Unitarian Univeralist Church		
	Hayward, CA	2-01-98
444.Taylor Memorial Methodist Church	Oakland, CA	10-27-96
445.Temple de la Cruz Church	Hayward, CA	9-22-96
446.Temple of Hope	San Leandro, CA	1-16-00
447.Temple United Methodist Church	San Francisco, CA	8-22-99
448.The Bridge	San Francisco, CA	11-14-99
449.The Jade Emperor's Palace (Buddhist)		
	San Francisco, CA	10-12-97
450.The Pentecostals Church	Hayward, CA	3-29-97
451.The World Is Life Deliverance Church		
	Snyder, TX	10-24-99
452.Third Baptist Church	San Francisco, CA	8-09-98
453.Thornton Avenue Baptist Church	Fremont, CA	6-02-96
454.Tibetan System of Healing	Berkeley, CA	5-18-97
455.Tri-City Baptist Church	Dublin, CA	6:22-97
456.Tri Cities Religious Science	Fremont, CA	7-13-97
457.Trinity Baptist Church	Livermore, CA	5-10-98
458.Trinity Cathedral	Sacramento, CA	8-20-00
459.Trinity Center	Walnut Creek, CA	10-31-99
460.Trinity Church of the Pines	Grand Lake, CO	3-22-98
461.Trinity Episcopal Church	Castro Valley, CA	6-14-98
462.Trinity Episcopal Church	Sacramento, CA	2-23-97
463.Trinity Lutheran	Pleasanton, CA	l0-03-99
464.Trinity Lutheran	Walnut Creek, CA	10-31-99
465.Twin Towers United Methodist Church		
	Alameda, CA	5-03-98
466.Unitarian Universalist Church	Livermore, CA	3-29-98
467.Unitarian Universalist Church	San Mateo, CA	12-26-99
468.United Church of Christ	Hayward, CA	1-31-99
469.United Methodist Church	Burlingame, CA	2-07-99
470.United Methodist Church	Fremont, CA	5-05-96
471.United Methodist Church	Burke, VA	7-02-00
472.United Methodist Church	Concord, CA	12-19-99
473.United Methodist Church	Los Altos, CA	12-05-99
474.United Methodist Church	Walnut Creek, CA	8-15-99

475. United Methodist Resurrection Church		
	Leawood, KS	7-18-99
476. Unity Center	Walnut Creek, CA	10-31-99
477. Unity Church	Castro Valley, CA	2-28-99
478. Unity Church	Fremont, CA	5-04-97
479. Unity Headquarters	Lees Summit, MO	7-25-99
480. University Lutheran Chapel	Berkeley, CA	8-30-98
481. Uptown Church of Christ	San Francisco, CA	7-04-99
482. Valley Baptist Church	Castro Valley, CA	2-27-00
483. Valley Baptist Church	San Rafael, CA	5-23-99
484. Valley Bible Church	Hercules, CA	2-13-00
485. Valley Bible Church	Pleasanton, CA	3-12-00
486. Valley Christian Center	Dublin, CA	1-23-00
487. Valley Community Church	Pleasanton, CA	7-16-00
488. Village Baptist	San Lorenzo, CA	3-24-96
489. Village Church	Prairie Village, KS	7-18-99
490. Vineyard Christian Fellowship	San Jose, CA	8-17-97
491. Vineyard Community Church	Livermore, CA	4-25-99
492. Visitation Parish	Kansas City, MO	7-24-99
493. Walnut Creek Friends Church	Walnut Creek, CA	3-30-97
494. Walnut Creek Presbyterian Church	Walnut Creek, CA	12-29-96l
495. Wesley United Methodist Church	Hayward, CA	3-28-97
496. West Portal Lutheran Church	San Francisco, CA	2-09-97
497. Western Hills Church	San Mateo, CA	4-18-99
498. Westminster Hills Presbyterian Church		
	Hayward, CA	10-18-98
499. World Is Life Deliverance Church	Snyder, TX	10-24-99
500. World Wide Church of God	San Leandro, CA	1-22-00
501. Zion Fellowship	Danville, CA	8-02-98
502. Zion Lutheran Church	Piedmont, CA	7-23-00
503. Zion Lutheran Church	San Francisco, CA	5-17-98

About the Author

Sidney Stone is a retired Baptist minister, still available for speeches, counseling, and weddings. The First Baptist Church of Livermore, California was his last pastorate.

He received a Bachelor of Arts degree from Ottawa (Kansas) University where he was selected for inclusion in the 1948-49 Who's Who Among Students in American Universities and Colleges. His Master of Theology degree was from Berkeley Baptist Divinity School in Berkeley, California.

Mr. Stone is a published writer and poet whose work is included in anthologies published by Infinity Limited and also in the 2000 edition of the *International Library of Poetry Anthology.* One of his poems is in *The Best Poems and Poets of 2001* (ISBN D-7951-5174-8).

He was the winner of the nationwide writing contest sponsored by Grand Auto stores. He has managed writing contests involving junior and senior high school students in both public and private schools in California.

ORDER FORM

1001 Fresh Ideas for Your Church

Your name:____

Church:____

Address:____

City:___________________ State:______ Zip:__________

Phone Number:____________________________________

E-mail:____

Number of books ordered:__________

Amount enclosed:__________________
(Please make checks payable to Petros Publishers)

Price each, \$14.95 plus \$3.00 shipping/handling=&17.95
California orders add \$1.25 sales tax=\$19.20
Canada, price each, \$19.95 plus \$3.00 s/h=\$22.95
For quantity discounts or questions, call 510-886-7973

Petros Publishers
P.O. Box 154
Hayward CA 94543
510-886-7973